To the Nines

Anthony Pioppi

SPORTS
MEDIA
GROUP

All inquiries should be addressed to:
Sports Media Group
An imprint of Ann Arbor Media Group, LLC
2500 S. State Street
Ann Arbor, MI 48104

Pioppi, Anthony, 1963-
   Nines : the heart of American golf / Anthony Pioppi.
      p. cm.
   Includes bibliographical references.
   ISBN-13: 978-1-58726-274-6 (hardcover : alk. paper)
   ISBN-10: 1-58726-274-6 (hardcover : alk. paper)
   1. Golf courses—United States—History. I. Title.

GV981.P57 2006
796.35206'873—dc22
2006013398

ISBN 13: 978-1-58726-274-6
ISBN 10: 1-58726-274-6
10 9 8 7 6 5 4 3 2 1

Printed and bound by Edwards Brothers, Inc., Ann Arbor, Michigan USA.

To Genevieve and Nerio, my mother and father

To Randy Smith for taking the time to talk with me about writing, golf, hockey, and the ponies, and in the process teaching me about life.

In memory of Ciara McDermott

Contents

Foreword

Back in the mid-seventies, when I was fourteen or fifteen, my dad was working for the Fall River (Mass.) Gas Company, which had a membership at—where else?—the Fall River Country Club. The course was a nine-hole gem designed by a little-known architect named Arthur Fenn, considered to be the first American-born golf professional. It was my initiation into nine-hole layouts.

One summer day at Fall River, Dad left me with my golfing buddy Mike Corrigan, and we made six trips around the layout before the sun set. We didn't discuss the elephant-hole-sized crater to the left of the fairway on Number 1 or the strategy of the layup at the par-5 second, but we loved the punchbowl green at the third hole, where we realized aiming anywhere near the bull's eye on the pole above the green on that blind second shot would get the ball somewhere on the middle of that putting surface.

My mind was more into my score and hitting shots than dissecting what the architect was thinking when he chose the tee and green sites, but I still learned what quirky was, that a blind shot is only blind once and that you could use terrain to move the golf ball.

Being by the river, the wind howled and, as a result, the course was challenging every day.

Back then, playing a nine-hole course was not considered strange. There is an abundance of them in New England. Actually, a lot of people preferred to play the nine-holers in our area, and many companies had their twilight leagues at nine-hole tracks, but that has changed.

Being a native Rhode Islander, I was fortunate to be in the neighborhood of some of the best Classical-era courses in the country: Rhode Island Country Club, where I caddied; historic Newport Country Club; and Wannamoisett Country Club, home of the prestigious Northeast Amateur. All were nearby.

Donald Ross was a household name to even the non-golfer. He summered in Little Compton, Rhode Island, where he had designed the seaside Sakonnet Golf Club, which opened in 1921. Other famous architects, including Willie Park, Seth Raynor, and Albert Tillinghast, had their hand in designing Rhode Island courses. But I still loved Fall River.

My parents were golfers and instilled in me a love and respect for the game that I carry with me today. They taught me the difference between a good golf course and a great one, and they were quite sure that a golf course or country club wasn't a bad place to drop a teenager off for the day.

If we fast-forward to the twenty-first century, it seems like the nine-hole course is a little like steel club shafts and Bull's-Eye putters—they are still out there, but you have to look for them.

Anthony Pioppi's *To the Nines* will likely change your perspective on nine-hole golf courses if you think of them as inferior, or reinvigorate your love if you are already a fan. He has researched some of the country's best and reveals their history in a manner that will get you off the couch, grabbing your clubs and finding out where the nearest one is to your home. The history of the famous and not-so-famous architects and their nine holes makes you wonder why, in today's land-strapped business of golf course design, most of today's designers haven't built one.

I have been fortunate to have played George Thomas's Marion Golf Course and Ross's Whitinsville. I've visited Highland Links Golf Course and walked T. Suffern Tailer's land in Newport; they are great pieces of America's golf history.

With *To the Nines,* you will not only feel the shots, the holes and the courses Anthony describes, but you will also get caught up in their unique and intriguing stories, all the while trying to figure out how you are going to get in your next nine holes.

Brad Faxon

Introduction

The modern golfer has been conditioned to believe that in order for a course to achieve greatness, it must be able to host a major tournament, be longer than 7,200 yards from the tips, and play to a par of 72. A waterfall is always a bonus.

In our quest to get to such perfect sites, we speed past courses that fit none of the criteria yet deserve our attention. Some of those layouts have only nine holes, yet are worthy of being called great.

In truth, nine-holers are an integral part of golf history in the United States. The first U.S. Amateur and U.S. Open were played at Newport Country Club's nine. Myopia Hunt Club in Massachusetts hosted one of the first U.S. Opens over nine holes, and out on Long Island, Shinnecock Hills Golf Club also started as nine. Most of the great designers of the classic era (before 1960) of architecture laid out top class nine-hole courses.

Of the approximately 17,000 golf courses in the United States, about 4,700 are regulation nine holes, yet most golfers have history on a nine-hole course, usually during the formative years of their games. Nine states have more nine-hole layouts than those with eighteen. Not surprisingly, seven are in the Plains States. Maine and Alaska are the exceptions.

In the modern era (after 1959), very few stellar nine-hole designs have been created, while most architects of the classic era have a number of nines to their credit. The design firm run by Jack Nicklaus has built more than 230 courses in more than twenty countries since the early 1970s, and not one is just nine holes.

I have a deep affinity for nine-holers that goes back to the birth of my love for the game. My first time on a golf course came on the nine-hole Cohasse Country Club in my hometown of Southbridge, Massachusetts. I was about five, and my grandmother was babysitting me on that warm summer day. She took me to her club—a 1916 Donald Ross design—in an effort to entertain me and at the same time to be able to visit with the friends that played through.

There I was, traipsing along as my Nona rode alongside in one of those three-wheel golf carts steered by a metal bar. I flailed away for what seemed like hours under a broiling sun, never getting a shot airborne.

The first bona fide round I ever played also came at a nine-holer, Woodstock (Connecticut) Golf Course, a quirky layout whose beginnings date back to the late 1890s.

My cousin Ronnie had agreed to take me. I was perhaps eleven or twelve, and I had been banging balls with an 8-iron around the backyard of my Aunt Josie and Uncle Pop's house with such enthusiasm—and only one broken window—that somebody figured it was time to get me out there for real. I thought Ronnie was the height of cool. He was about ten years older than me, drove a VW bug, had played college football, and loved golf.

Woodstock is a quirky layout, and at the time it was a barebones operation that included dirt tees. There are a number of blind shots and tiny greens, design features sneered at by a majority of modern golfers but ones that we found entertaining.

Our favorite green from that day no longer exists—a natural punchbowl design that would have made course architects who are fans of the style (such as Seth Raynor, Pete Dye, or Brian Silva) dance with glee. Years later somebody decided to try to outsmart nearly a hundred years of success by moving the green back twenty yards onto a plateau, in the process converting a charming green into an ordinary one.

Ronnie and I putted the original for a good ten minutes, completely enthralled with the wild turns and breaks the ball took even back then, when the grass was probably mowed to a quarter of an inch.

Maybe it is because of Woodstock that I have such a love of unusual layouts, the kind I want to play again and again.

There was also Hemlock Golf Course in Sturbridge, where I often played as a kid.

It was a mom-and-pop operation run by the family that designed and built the place. The owners at the time were ornery, no matter how many rounds we played, hot dogs we ate, or golf balls we deposited in the pond that made their way to the used ball jar.

It is being kind to say the majority of Hemlock's holes are not very good, yet in the middle of these design faux pas sits a 320-yard, par-4, downhill, dogleg-left slice of brilliance.

For those who can turn the ball slightly right to left with some power, the hole was drivable even in the early 1980s. For those who can't, it demands a well-placed layup.

In the middle of the fairway the approach is from a severe downhill lie. Since at the time we were playing golf balls with the consistency of granite and were incapable of applying backspin, the ideal second shot would land short of the green, catch a sharp downslope, and disappear for what seemed like a lifetime before emerging on the putting surface.

A shot hit too hard would roll off the severely sloped green and tumble away, usually into the thick underbrush.

Without even knowing it we were playing links-style golf, using the bump-and-run on a hole that required thought and offered options from tee to green.

There have been other nine-holers in my life since then. For the two and a half years I lived on the seacoast of New Hampshire, Sunningdale Golf Course was my home base. I've been in Connecticut for nearly twenty years, and although I've played most of my golf at eighteen-holers, Fenwick Golf Course in Old Saybrook earned a special place in my heart from the first time my friend Joe D'Ambrosio took me there. No matter how bad the mood I'm in on the first tee at Fenwick, it never seems to take more than a few swings for that to change.

In my heart, though, Cohasse remains my favorite. I have the memories with my grandmother, but more recent ones as well. My parents were bitten anew by the golf bug and became members.

I know Cohasse as well as any course I've played, and the talent of Ross reveals itself each time I'm out there. It is a primer in thoughtful design, where par is a good score on any hole but shorter hitters can find routes to tack their way around trouble and enjoy the day—something that can't always be said about championship layouts playing 7,500 yards. I only wish the members would take it upon themselves to restore the layout to Ross's original plans.

From Massachusetts's mill towns to Tennessee's Cumberland Plateau, to a California national park and everywhere in between, exceptional nine-hole golf courses abound. Golfers just need to slow down a little and find them. It will be worth the trip.

Highland Links

A Gem in the Far East

HISTORIANS SAY AFTER THE TRYING winter voyage of 1620, the Pilgrims first dropped anchor off what is now Truro, Massachusetts, on Cape Cod, before moving on down the coast to the famous rock and what became Plymouth.

More than two hundred years later, Henry David Thoreau, walking Cape Cod from one end to the other, spent the night in a small lodge on a bluff in Truro run by James and Jerusha Small and declared the location ideal for a resort.

"A man can stand here and put all of America behind him," wrote Thoreau.

Since 1797, when it was built, the Small family had been involved with the keeping of the Cape's first lighthouse, Highland Light. Isaac M. Small started the Highland House resort in 1907, when he realized the area was becoming a popular vacation destination and the only lodging was in town. He also took over the marine telegraph station adjacent to the lighthouse, and from that vantage point Small sent news of ship sightings on to Boston so the port could prepare for the arrivals. He was also a correspondent for a number of news organizations, including the *Boston Globe,* newspapers on the Cape, and the Associated Press, to which he reported news from the tip of the peninsula, including the all-too-common shipwrecks.

Isaac opened the resort and, in the last decade of the 1800s, helped to create a nine-hole golf course on one of the most spectacular sites anywhere in the United States, with views like no other.

Highland Links Golf Course is perched on a bluff some 130 feet above the Atlantic and inside the Cape Cod National Seashore. It is the only course with such a distinction.

1

The Cape Cod Light is omnipresent during a round at Highland Links. Here it stands sentinel over the short, testing par-3 ninth that was said to have inspired Donald Ross but, in fact, could not have; it was built after his death in 1948. (Photograph by ENELYSION/George Ruhe)

Small greens and wispy, knee-deep rough defining wide-open fairways all whisper "links-style golf" to every player willing to listen. The unremitting winds coming off Cape Cod Bay to the west or the Atlantic to the east boldly announce this jewel, which comes in at about 2,650 yards and with a par of 35 that is no patsy. Perched just off the course, keeping watch over it all, is Cape Cod Light.

In 1912, Isaac M. Small published a pamphlet for visitors to Highland Resort and the lighthouse, setting the scene and the mood of the bluff where the course was built:

> *Stretching as it does, far out into the ocean, fanned by the cool breezes of the Atlantic, and the milder winds that float across the smooth waters of the bay; with an unobstructed view of the horizon, where the sun is in full view from the moment it rises in the east until it sets in the west.*

On this dot of seashore is a course of quirks and challenges with a disputed and a somewhat murky history.

Highland House Golf Links

THESE Links in attractiveness are not equalled on the New England coast. The gently rolling moors and the beautiful sea, ever in view, make the course a charm to the eye and a delightful source of recreation and pleasure. It is a nine hole course, 2,000 yards around. These Links are often declared to be typical of the best golf courses in Scotland, which they greatly resemble. Francis Ouimet, Amateur Golf Champion of the United States, and France, has played on this course and was delighted with it. We are permitted to show this great player at points on the course. Good golfing by the beginning of April.

Highland House and Cottages
OCEAN SIDE CAPE COD, NORTH TRURO, MASS.

E. HAYES SMALL, LESSEE AND MANAGER

While Highland Links is the only golf course inside the U.S. National Seashore, it might also be the course that's gone through the most names. In this pamphlet the moniker switched to Highland House Golf Links. (Courtesy of Truro Historical Society, Inc.)

The story around the small clubhouse and across the wide-open layout is that Highland Links opened for play in 1892 for people who were staying at the lighthouse keeper's cottage or in the small summer homes that dotted the area—making it one of the ten oldest courses in the country and the oldest on the Cape—and that the layout has remained relatively unchanged since its inception. None of those assertions—the 1892 founding, oldest course on the Cape, or that it has remained untouched for over a century—appears to be true, but the facts of the course's history do not diminish its character and ambiance.

The 1892 number has long been treated as suspect by golf historians. There appears to be no connection between the Small family and any of the other courses or golfers of the era on the Cape; no record of a Scottish relative, clubs in hand, making his way across the Atlantic and to the Highlands. In addition, how a family that for three generations lived almost sixty miles from Boston came to the game far ahead of almost the entire country cannot be explained.

In 1993, National Park Service historian Larry Lowenthal, also not believing the 1892 date, set out find its origin. It was then he came across the pamphlet "A Little About the Lower Cape," published in 1922 by Isaac M. Small, who was running the resort and the lighthouse. In the pamphlet, which was sold to guests and tourists, Small stated that the course was laid out "in 1892 by my son Willard, relaid by me in 1913 from plans by Mr. J. H. McKinley of New York."

Lowenthal discovered that, when reprinting the pamphlet fourteen years later, Small removed any mention of the year 1892, although the golf course was still described at length. Another edition published after Small's death also contained nothing about the 1892 date.

Further digging by Lowenthal into town records led him to believe that Highland Links was founded in 1898. Although there is no definitive proof, the date makes more sense: by that time golf was making its way from the city out to the Cape, where the first nine holes were built in Yarmouthport in 1893. That course no longer exists. In the neighboring town of Barnstable, the original nine holes of Cummaquid Golf Club— later expanded to eighteen holes—opened in 1898.

The second myth was debunked in the early 1990s, when Lillian M. Small, granddaughter of Isaac Small, who had lived at Highland House and golfed at the course, returned to the area from her home in Florida.

During her brief visit, she sketched out her recollection of the second incarnation of the course—stating that it was designed by frequent hotel guest McKinley in 1913.

In its earliest days the course conditions at Highland Links were spotty at best but the allure of playing on a bluff some forty feet above the Atlantic Ocean was enough to draw golfers, including Francis Ouimet. (Courtesy of Truro Historical Society, Inc.)

Other changes occurred throughout the 1900s, including a rerouting by Henry Conklin, who had bought Highland House—which included the golf course—in 1946, becoming the first person other than a Small family member to run the resort since it was founded. The National Park Service acquired the property in 1964, and the town of Truro has run the course since.

Not all the alterations were bad. In his research, Lowenthal discovered that at one point, eight of the greens were sand while the putting surface for the seventh—probably located at the beginning of the current second fairway—was for unknown reasons made of concrete covered with sand.

It is possible that many of the hole corridors are the same as those of the first routing, but although some of the green sites are in original locations, none of the holes are as they were in the 1890s. For instance, the green of the par-3 seventh hole is in the exact location where the putting surface for the original par-4 first sat.

The biggest change that occurred with the Conklin rerouting was the positioning of the eighth and ninth holes on the north side of Highland Road, located on land that was the longtime vegetable garden for the Highland House kitchen.

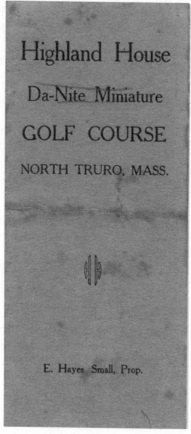

Through the years Highland House offered a number of other activities for its guests in addition to golf. At one time, miniature golf was played although no remnants of the layout remain and parts of the regular course doubled as a baseball diamond. (Courtesy of Truro Historical Society, Inc.)

That configuration of holes was probably changed as a result of the march of time, which on that part of the Cape can move rapidly.

The lighthouse has been a part of the course since its inception, but even more so since 1996, when it was relocated some 450 feet inland to the eroding bluff, which loses as much as forty feet a year to the Atlantic Ocean. The last rerouting of the holes occurred for the same reason. The repositioning of the working lighthouse moved it closer to the course.

It is not the only structure in the history of Highland Links with a connection to the sea. In 1915, the tugboat Mars was wrecked below the cliffs of the Highland property while towing three barges, one of them the *Coleraine*. The deckhouse from that grounded barge was salvaged and moved near the golf course, where it first became an annex to the hotel and later was used as a bar until it was demolished in the 1950s.

The course opens with a par 4 of 250 yards, drivable even without a tailwind thanks to the firm turf, but a miscue long can result in a quick double bogey to start the day.

The 460-yard, par-5 second starts with a tee ball that drops 30 feet to a fairway, then takes golfers through a natural cut into the sand dunes with the Jenny Lind Tower watching them all. Originally part of the Fitchburg Railway depot in Boston, the tower was moved to Truro in 1927 by Henry Aldrich when the depot was demolished. Aldrich was a fan of the famous opera singer Jenny Lind, known as the Swedish Nightingale. As the story goes, she was booked to perform in the hall above the station and is reputed to have sung from the fifty-five-foot, medieval-style tower to quell an imminent riot of fans unable to attend the performance, which was oversold by promoter P. T. Barnum.

Next to the tower sits a radar dome left over from a World War II–era flight surveillance station.

After a deceptive, trying uphill par 3, those playing Highland for the first time would best forget the scorecard and enjoy the views. The next three holes work their way back and forth over the wind-whipped Moors land. The views are fantastic, with none better than that from the tee of the 464-yard, par-5 sixth that sits on the edge of the 130-foot bluff, offering a sweeping vista of the ocean and golf course. The slight dogleg right is a bear with or against the wind.

The course finishes 3-4-3, with the ninth surely one of the best short holes anywhere and the subject of another unfounded Highland Links tale.

The tee is flush against what was the back door of the Highland House, now the Truro Historical Society, with a two-tiered green waiting 136 yards in the distance. A gnarly edged bunker guards the right half of the putting surface, which lies a good three feet higher than the left. And, in picture-book fashion, Highland Light stands sentinel over it all.

The official course history says the hole inspired the legendary course architect Donald Ross in his building of short threes, but that is impossible. Ross died in 1948. The earliest the hole was constructed was 1955.

Myths be damned. Highland Links does not need them to elevate its status. It stands as a wonderful test of golf skill in an unparalleled setting and remains one of the finest nine-hole courses in the country.

Marion

The Forgotten Debut of George Thomas

George Thomas had plenty to be proud of in his life. He was a world-renowned rose grower and sport fisherman, writing definitive books about those subjects. He also was a soldier who bravely served his country in World War I—he was shot down three times in a year of duty and used his own money to outfit his squad. An accomplished golf course architect with such notable layouts to his name as Riviera Country Club, Thomas never charged a fee for his work. He also authored what is still considered by many—nearly ninety years after its publication—to be the bible of design, *Golf Architecture in America.*

Yet apparently, the Captain—as he was known after his war years—had a skeleton in his golfing closet. The cause of his embarrassment was his first-ever design, a nine-holer called Marion Golf Course, located just east of Plymouth, Massachusetts.

In his 342-page book, Thomas used more than ninety course drawings and fifty photos of his work and that of others to illustrate what he believed to be sound golf holes. Yet he devotes a mere five lines to Marion. This short paragraph raises more questions than answers. He offered little understanding about how he was chosen for the job, about his thinking behind the design of the holes, and about who, if anyone, was his main influence.

"The first course I ever constructed by myself was for a small club sponsored by the well-off William Bullivant ["King Tut"] of Marion, Massachusetts. I have often wondered why he trusted me, and admired his sportsmanship for doing so." That's it. Not another word. Not another reference. Yet Thomas thought so highly of another course in Marion that he included a photo and drawing of the third hole at the Kittansett Club—not just located in the same town as his course, but also on the same road. In fact, one must drive past Marion to get to Kittansett.

Thomas did such a good job concealing his role that for years his association with the sporty layout was forgotten. The current lessors of the course, Sue and Bruce Carlson, unearthed the nugget while researching the history shortly after taking over the operation in the early 1990s. (A trust originally established by Bullivant oversees the golf course.) It can be safely said that there is no other golf architect in America of Thomas's stature whose debut work has been forgotten. The respective fans of Thomas contemporaries such as Donald Ross, Perry Maxwell, Charles Blair Macdonald, and Seth Raynor can easily name the first work of each without hesitation

The best guess is that the course opened sometime between 1904 and 1907. Thomas's second design—Whitemarsh Valley Country Club outside Philadelphia—opened in 1908. The connection between Thomas and Bullivant may have been King Tut's grandson, William "Mac" Bullivant, who was an avid sailor and apparently an awful golfer, and most likely a friend of Thomas.

At the time, Marion was home to many wealthy families and a summer resort community for the elite. Grover Cleveland, the twenty-second and twenty-fourth president of the United States, vacationed there, as did actors such as Lyle Barrymore. The Delanos—as in Franklin Delano Roosevelt—were a prominent Marion family.

The Bullivants were also large landowners in the town, with the family fortune coming via ownership of the Northeast Leather Company outside of Boston.

A scrapbook once belonging to Mac Bullivant, and which now is in the hands of his grandnephew, Willliam Maurice Bullivant III, is full of newspaper clippings from the 1910 Buzzards Bay sailboat-racing season off the southern Massachusetts coast. Competing in the second division of the Sonder Boat class, Mac racked up an impressive year, finishing in the top three in a number of races and taking home a goodly number of titles. George C. Thomas Jr. also raced, but was near the bottom of nearly every listing of race finishers.

Golf, however, may be the great equalizer. A scorecard, found in the scrapbook and dated September 11, 1910, is the oldest known artifact of the course and offers up a tantalizing clue. On that day, Bullivant carded a 14 on the easy par-4 first on his

William Bullivant III stands in front of a portrait of his great grandfather William "King Tut" Bullivant, who gave George Thomas the opportunity to design his first golf course. Bullivant holds a family album that contains a 1910 Marion scorecard. (Photograph by Anthony Pioppi)

way to a score of 70-71–141; a 107 with his handicap of 34 figured in. Whoever was Bullivant's opponent that day—Thomas perhaps?—opened with a par 4, and that is where the scoring for Bullivant's companion stops. Thomas was in the area at the time. A day later the pair sailed in a Sonder race, with the results from the local paper clipped and stored in the scrapbook.

Or perhaps there is a romantic connection. Under the handwritten title of Marion 1910 is a collection of photographs. Three snapshots of a smiling woman only identified as E. Thomas are found, and in each she is holding what appears to be a stuffed animal, possibly a dog. They are the only photos of just the woman, though she appears in group photos as well. Is this Thomas's sister, and could she have been fancied by Mac Bullivant?

The Captain was fifteen years older than Mac, but his sister was the same age. Although Mac did not marry until years later, it appears he might well have had his eye on the Captain's sister.

The man who enlisted Thomas to build the course would die much less wealthy than he was when he bequeathed the land to be used for golf. King Tut lost everything in the stock market crash. In Bullivant family annals, however, he is held in great esteem, sacrificing his own fortune to pay off every last one of his creditors, doling out $3 million—equivalent to roughly $75 million today—over a six-month period.

However, his son Stewart Lodge ran the course for a number of years. Longtime regulars remember him always dressed in a coat and tie and, without hesitation, forbidding someone from playing if he did not like the person's appearance or attitude. But it is also said that if Stewart was leaving for the day, he would often leave a lit lamp on the bunker wall fronting the ninth green as a target for those playing the final hole in the dark.

What made Thomas turn his back on his initial foray into the architecture field may not be difficult to figure out. Even though Marion is a fun layout that presents a myriad of design features and can test even low-handicappers, especially with a breeze coming off bordering Buzzards Bay, it fails to meet many of the criteria for a solid course Thomas set down in his book, which was published some twenty years after the layout opened.

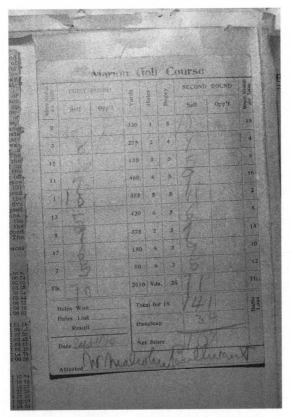

In the midst of a scrapbook filled with newspaper clippings and photos involving William "Mac" Bullivant is a scorecard from Marion dated Sept. 11, 1910. It is the oldest known artifact from a course whose opening date is unknown. (Photograph by Anthony Pioppi)

As he looked back at Marion through educated eyes, its foibles must have seemed glaring to Thomas. By the time of the book's publication, he was considered one of the best architects in the country, as evidenced by the fact he was invited to add his ideas to the design of the legendary Pine Valley Golf Club in New Jersey.

Reasons for Thomas's disdain for Marion might be found in *Architects of Golf,* in which the chapter "The Strategy of the Golf Course" sets out conditions for the ideal layout.

For instance, Thomas came to the conclusion that putting played an important role in the game, and that it was up to the architect to reveal that skill through green design. He wrote that it is "absolutely necessary that the greens be properly built so the greatest amount of skill be insisted upon in the use of this club."

At Marion, even with current green speeds, which Thomas never could have imagined, the small, flattish putting surfaces do not call for much skill. Only the inverted saucer of the wild second requires any sort of deft touch.

Thomas had also formulated a strong opinion on the role of par: "Pars are for nearly perfect play, not for puny drives or wild tee shots, unless, after such, the player makes fine recoveries or holes out in one putt." Later he added: "The poorest of all holes are the short two-shotters, where a missed first shot allows a recovery to the green that is only a mediocre shot."

Unfortunately, the first hole at Marion violates both these conditions. At 315 yards, it has a blind green set in a hollow that could easily be drivable were it not for two bunkers set into the fairway at the point where it begins sloping toward the green, some forty yards from the putting surface. Because of the bunkers' placement, all strategy is lost. Certainly one can try to run a tee shot through the sand, but the only logical play is to lay up, leaving a short approach.

A missed tee shot, however, is no cause for alarm, for even an indifferent second shot—even a downright awful second—that manages to clear the bunkers will bound its way down the slope and onto the green or, at worst, very near it.

When Thomas wrote that "hazards should not unduly penalize," he must have blotted from his mind the defining feature of Marion: stone walls.

Present on nearly every hole, they run perpendicular and parallel to the line of play, causing trouble for well-struck and duffed shots alike. Balls can lodge in the gaps of the stones, leaving no chance of recovery and only a penalty drop as escape. Although it has never been documented that Thomas visited courses in the British Isles during his post–World War I service, the walls conjure up images of courses such as the West Links at North Berwick, Scotland, and Ardglass in Northern Ireland, where stone walls are a dominant and enjoyable component.

There are three par 3s at Marion, all blind off the tee thanks to stone walls. On the eighth hole a small opening allows golfers a direct path to the green 180 yards from the tee. (Photograph by Geoff Shackelford)

Again, when Thomas came to the last part of the chapter, he must have cringed while penning these words: "One properly made blind or semi-blind green is permissible... Too many of these holes are to be avoided." He added that "if such a blind green is of the punchbowl type, it is more satisfactory."

When Thomas suggested that one blind green on a course was permissible, he was referring to an eighteen-hole layout. At Marion, four of the holes are blind or partially obscured, including all three one-shotters.

One of these, however, Thomas might still have appreciated. The ninth is a downhill 115-yarder, with a large bunker built into the remnants of what Marion historian Paul Boutin believes is a stone coral, obscuring a shallow concave green and creating a wonderful blind punchbowl. The tee is backed into another high, arced stone wall that borders the Bunker, King Tut's home at the time of course construction.

But even though Marion fails to meet Thomas's own standards for what makes a great course, it passes a test he did not mention—it is high on the fun factor. In this category, Marion receives accolades.

On one hand, Marion is museum piece existing much as it did when it opened more than a hundred years ago. At the same time, it is a joy to play, the golfing equivalent of driving a genuine Model T. You won't be cruising in the fast lane, but, oh, will the ride be a blast.

Part of what makes it so enjoyable is Thomas's willingness to experiment with a variety of architecture styles, giving Marion its unique character. It was as if Thomas were trying to incorporate every design feature he could think of in the 2,695-yard course. Heroic, penal, and strategic bunkering find their ways into the layout. There's no fairway irrigation, so the turf is firm enough to permit the playing of the ground game much as Thomas envisioned it the day the course opened.

Most of the green surfaces are at or near their original dimensions, and the one bunker anyone can ever remember being added to the course was removed during the mid-1980s, less than ten years after it had been built. It appears that only one original bunker has been lost to time.

Thomas learned how to golf at Essex County Club and the Myopia Club, both on Boston's North Shore and both designed by Herbert Leeds. At Essex, Thomas would have played the course before Donald Ross redesigned it. When it expanded from nine to eighteen holes, club records say, Leeds had a hand in helping the team of Walter Travis and John Duncan Dunn lay out the new course, where dynamite was used for the first time in golf course construction—such a novelty in those days it was reported on by the British press. While playing Essex and Myopia, Thomas would have undoubtedly rubbed shoulders with U.S. President William Howard Taft, who from 1909 to 1912 summered in nearby Beverly, Massachusetts, playing golf at both courses.

What Thomas would have learned from Essex can only be guessed, for the course from that era is all but gone. The only hole remaining is the long par-5 third that dates to the original nine. The most unforgettable feature of the third is a bathtub-sized depression in the left side of the green. Maybe that in-green hazard crept into Thomas's unconscious and lay dormant, only to come to the surface years later when he designed a bunker in the middle of the sixth green at Riviera.

Myopia, on the other hand, remains much the way it was when Thomas played it. By 1908, Myopia had hosted four U.S.

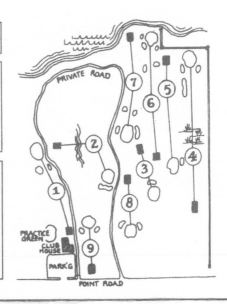

COURSE RATING 67
SLOPE RATING 116

U.S.G.A. RULES APPLY

PLEASE REPLACE ALL DIVOTS

DO NOT GO INTO FIELDS ON #4 AND #6

ETIQUETTE

- RAKE BUNKERS
- REPAIR BALL MARKS
- REPLACE DIVOTS
- ALLOW FASTER GROUPS THROUGH
- PROPER golf attire must be required at all times

PRIVATE ROAD

POINT ROAD

MARION GOLF COURSE

POINT ROAD, MARION, MA 02738

PLAY AT OWN RISK!

The Marion Golf Course of today is nearly identical to the one that is the debut work of George Thomas designed in the first decade of the 1900s. Stone walls accent the quirky layout on which Thomas used myriad green styles.

Opens—including the only one ever contested over a nine-hole course—and was considered the first golf layout in the United States that could stand up to its European counterparts as a true test of golf.

Here Thomas may have learned his green designs. Although the fairways of Myopia roll, tumble, and tilt, the greens are flat, relying on pitch to create challenging situations. And they did, even with the slow green speeds of the early 1900s. In 1908, for instance, Ernie Way putted off the fourth green and into a swamp, losing his ball. A bunker added years later now prevents that from happening again.

Wherever Thomas found his inspiration for Marion, it seems not to have been enough to please him when he looked back years later. Yet Marion is enjoyed to this day, providing enjoyment to thousands of golfers a year. In that light, how can the debut work of Thomas be considered anything less than a success?

Whitinsville

The Reigning Champion

Whitinsville Golf Club does something few other highly touted layouts can do—it lives up to its reputation.

If Whitinsville is not the greatest nine-hole course in the country, it surely resides in the rarefied air of the top three. It is a Donald Ross gem, located in Central Massachusetts, that displays shades and hues reminiscent of other New England Ross standouts, such as Rhode Island Country Club and Essex County Club in Massachusetts.

The course is spacious off the tee, but dastardly on approaches that require pinpoint accuracy followed by a deft putting stroke. Greens will be missed, so to score well a superlative short game is required.

Ross was provided with a sixty-nine-acre canvas, much of which had for years been tilled as farmland—making earth moving that much easier. The site is replete with rolling topography and a profusion of wonderful views of the Mumford River.

For much of Whitinsville's existence, other courses such as the former Ocean Links in Rhode Island, Prairie Dunes Country Club in Kansas, and Rolling Rock Club in Pennsylvania could lay claim to being the best nine-hole golf course in the country, but they all fell off the mountain. The last contender was eliminated in 1997 when Rolling Rock—another Ross layout—had Brian Silva add an additional nine that has thrilled the membership. Since that time, Whitinsville has, in the eyes of most architecture aficionados, assumed the crown.

Whitinsville was the quintessential small New England mill town when the Whitin family decided to build a golf course. For nearly a century, Whitin Machine Works had been the lifeblood of the community. The largest producer of textile machinery in the world, the company was located in the heart of the Blackstone River Valley, some twenty miles southeast of Worcester, Massachusetts, an area rich in textile manufacturing history. It was not too far away, in Slatersville, Rhode Island, that Henry Slater, father of the American Industrial Revolution, opened his first textile mill. Later he would devise what became known as the Rhode Island System, in which entire families worked in the factories and lived, shopped, learned, and prayed at company-controlled entities. In Whitinsville's case, they also golfed at the company course.

The yarn around the Whitinsville clubhouse to this day is that when the Whitin family approached Ross to build nine holes, he turned them down, saying he would only work on eighteen-hole projects.

At best, the tale is suspect. In 1925, Whitinsville and four other Ross nine-holers opened, and he designed nearly twenty other nine-hole courses that opened after 1925.

The Whitinsville scenario was nearly identical to one that occurred a decade earlier to the west of Worcester, in Southbridge, Massachusetts. The Wells family, owners of the American Optical Company, the largest manufacturer of eyeglasses in the world, hired Ross to build them nine holes. Cohasse Country Club opened in 1916. It is obvious that Ross or one of his associates spent much more time at Whitinsville than Cohasse, producing a layout with far more interesting greens and much more strategy.

According to the Whitinsville account, Ross changed his mind and agreed to build the course when he was allowed a free hand on two parcels of land separated by Fletcher Street. In the words of the *Whitin Spindle,* the official publication of Whitin Machine, "In laying out this course, Donald Ross was given carte blanche to make it the very last word in golf construction and it is in the general opinion that Mr. Ross had accomplished this result."

The par-35 layout was 3,163 yards long, with the first hole as the only par 5.

At Whitinsville, Ross saved the best for last, or, more accurately, saved one of his best ever for last.

The *Spindle* dedicated nearly all of its May–June 1925 issue to the course and described the finishing hole this way: "Number nine is considered by Mr. Ross as one of the best '2 shot' holes in the country."

Like other architects he often inflated his opinion of his own work, but here his review was on the mark. More than fifty years later, the ninth was picked as one of the 500 best holes in the country and among the very best Ross ever built. The par 4, which now plays between 416 and 446 yards, was 420 yards long when the course opened.

The hole is based on three plateaus: the tee, landing area, and green. The tee drops off some thirty feet to a neck of the Mumford, then back up to a large plateau. The hole doglegs right, with the fairway tumbling toward the river. A tee shot that flirts with danger presents the best approach angle, but an overplayed effort goes unforgiven, ending up in the Mumford.

The *Spindle* described the challenge, saying in part that "this is a water hole and will require a long straight drive to start, and if you slice it you're lost."

The fairway again drops off, rising sharply to a putting surface guarded on the left and right by bunkers, snug to the original clubhouse.

The Massachusetts-based Ross was so enamored with his design that when fellow architect George Thomas solicited drawings and photos for his treatise on course design, *Golf Architecture in America,* Ross submitted a drawing of the ninth at Whitinsville, which Thomas captioned thus: "A fine type of drive and full iron or spoon to the green. The high plateau is a most suitable landing place for a drive and gives unobstructed view of the green."

In 1988, when the U.S. Open came to The Country Club in nearby Brookline, Massachusetts, Ben Crenshaw was asked to pick his favorite Ross holes for a magazine article. Along with ones from Pinehurst No. 2 and Seminole, he selected the ninth at Whitinsville.

The ninth stands out, but the course abounds in stellar holes. It opens with a par 5 built on land that was once part of the Whitinsville Cotton Mill Farm. Clubhouse lore says that the area where the fairway sits was for many years the burial ground for horses from Whitin Machine. The hole bends to the left and placement on the first two shots is amply rewarded.

Next comes the downhill par-3 second at 137 yards. It is in classic Ross design style, with soil pushed up to form the green pad and then bunkers—in this case four—carved into the base. The back is unguarded by sand, but the putting surface drops

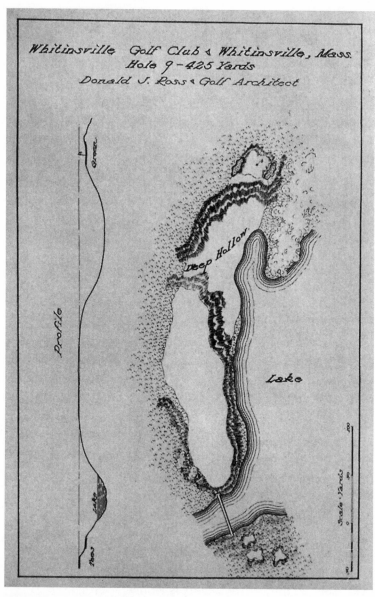

Whitinsville Golf Club & Whitinsville, Mass.
Hole 9 – 425 Yards
Donald J. Ross & Golf Architect

Whitinsville Golf Club finishes with a stunning par 4 in which Ross utilizes three plateaus along the Mumford River. Architect George Thomas included a drawing of the hole in his book *Golf Architecture in America*. Ben Crenshaw considers the 9th one of the finest par 4s in the country.

sharply as a defense against the overly aggressive effort. What appears as a relatively mundane one-shotter proves to be much more difficult, especially if the tee shot fails to find its target. The green is heart-shaped, rotated 90 degrees counterclockwise.

After crossing Fletcher Street for the medium length par 4s that are the third and fourth holes, players return to take on the first of three par 4s of more than 410 yards; the fifth is the longest at 440 yards and presents players with their only blind shot of the round.

Tee balls must carry a natural ridge, with a cluster of bunkers nestled on the inside of the dogleg right, only about 140 yards out but looking much more imposing. Those who do carry the ridge will catch a downslope propelling the shot farther down the fairway.

The fifth is backed up by the downhill 416-yard sixth, which was softened years ago when a brook some 25 yards in front of the green was covered over.

After the medium length par-3 seventh, Ross followed with a tantalizing effort on the eighth. Only 350 yards, the uphill, dogleg left is fraught with trouble. Shorter hitters can avoid the inlet of the Mumford River by playing away from the water, which creates a longer, more challenging approach. However, more aggressive players will find themselves wanting to gnaw off more of the carry and possibly challenge a bunker that awaits on the upslope of the fairway. Like its counterpart at No. 5, the green once afforded a wide view of the Mumford, but trees now obscure that. It is worth the time to take the short walk to the river's edge and admire the scenery.

It is interesting that the *Spindle* article also went into some detail on the construction of the course, especially the putting surfaces.

"All the greens and teeing grounds have been constructed in accordance with the most modern practice. The greens are well propped up at the rear to allow for bold pitching and vary in shape and contour." Then later: "All of the greens have been sown with creeping bent stolons, which method of raising grass has given excellent quick results with playable greens the first year after the stolons are put in."

Time and effort were put not only into the greens, but the rest of the course as well. The bunkering is evidence of this. It has long been suspected that Ross had little or nothing to do

The second hole is classic Donald Ross. It is a short par 3 surrounded by trouble; three bunkers carved out of the fill pad are an obvious problem to golfers. Not seen is a steeply banked back slope that sends errant shots tumbling away. (Photograph by Anthony Pioppi)

with Whitinsville beyond possibly the routing, and that J. B. McGovern was really the man behind the design.

Ross was busy in 1925 with eight projects—either new constructions or renovations—opening in Florida alone, including Sara Bay Country Club, where for a time Bobby Jones played golf with prospective home buyers in an effort to sell real estate that surrounded the course. The only documented meeting of Ross and Jones occurred on the Sara Bay site prior to construction.

It would be easy to assume that Ross neglected Whitinsville in favor of the Florida projects and other high-profile openings of 1925, such as Biltmore Forest Golf Club in western North Carolina. However, that most was likely not the case.

In November of 1924, Ross married Florence Blackinton; both had been widowed. Ross sold his summer home in Newton Center, moving into the Blackinton house in North Attleboro, Massachusetts, some forty-five miles from Whitinsville. In Sep-

Mounds covered in diabolical rough come into play on the sixth and eighth holes. Architect Donald Ross left the front of the eighth green free of any hazards but a good drive that flirts with disaster on the left results in a much shorter approach shot. (Photograph by Anthony Pioppi)

tember of 1925, he moved his summer office into the Blackinton summer house along the shore in Little Compton, on the far eastern tip of Rhode Island, where his Sakonnet Golf Club had opened in 1921. Even from there he was probably less than two hours from Whitinsville.

The strategy surely points to the hand of Ross. The first hole off the tee dares players to challenge bunkers on the left hand side that guard a speed slot. On the third hole, an artfully placed bunker some thirty yards short of the green all but obscures the putting surface. Those looking for the open route must flirt with the mounds and woods that guard the right side of the fairway.

The strategic design of those holes and the other seven suggests that Ross was at Whitinsville and is the biggest reason why the course stands as the best nine-holer in the country.

Ocean Links

The Brief, Glorious Life

Newport Country Club stands as one of the enduring images of golf in the United States, appearing much as it did some one hundred years ago—almost timeless in its simple beauty with its unirrigated fairways, rough-edged bunkers, and swaying grasses of gold and amber, all overseen by a stately clubhouse on the Rhode Island coastline.

Next door sit the remnants of Ocean Links, possibly the greatest nine-hole golf course ever in the United States. Through the seven-foot-high chain link fence that borders the west side of Newport CC, and across what was once Commonwealth Avenue, amidst the tangle of thorns, vines, and scrub brush, underneath open meadows, below soaring kites held hard against the vivid blue sky by a relentless ocean wind or in the midst of high-priced homes, is the decaying carcass of a layout whose ephemeral existence captivated the golfing world for a little more than ten years—a finger snap on the golf timeline.

This is no Pharaoh's tomb that if unearthed would reveal hidden treasures, but an ancient shipwreck, its priceless cargo scattered and all but lost, with only a handful of worn artifacts remaining to stimulate the imagination of what once was.

Long gone is the home and fishing club of Thomas Suffern Tailer, the man who conceived and funded the project and created the Gold Mashie Tournament played there—and whose sudden death at the Christmas dinner table ultimately led to its premature demise. On the land that once housed Ocean Links, a jewel in the world of golf course architecture, now sits a small state park and a few private homes. Where once the greatest amateur golfers of the day trod in pursuit of a vaunted title, ordinary folk sit and enjoy a peaceful place to relax.

What survives of Ocean Links is at times barely discernible—a few greens and tees may stand out to those looking for clues, but to most they are nothing more than mounds and rolls on which to lounge under a warm Rhode Island sun. They in no way resemble the massive undulated putting surfaces and gaping bunkers so artfully designed and built by Charles Blair Macdonald and Seth Raynor.

At other times, well-preserved remnants such as a fairway bunker survive in almost a comical form, sitting alone in the middle of a well-manicured yard and appearing more like a child's sandbox than a golf hazard, yet built by two of the finest architects ever.

Tailer was the only official member of Ocean Links, although members of Newport CC—of which Tailer was one—were granted access to the course. Among them was John Hayes, the Newport head golf professional for more than forty-five years.

Tailer's son, Thomas Suffern "Tommy" Tailer Jr., played at Ocean Links and Newport, honing a game that would lead him to become, at sixteen, the youngest participant in the U.S. Amateur up to that time. He also played in and made the cut of three Masters from 1938 to 1940.

One aerial photograph of Ocean Links is known to exist, and only because the layout was so close to Newport CC that it was inevitably included when Newport commissioned a photo of its course in 1929. The photo was most likely taken from one of the dirigibles that were tethered to a warship in Newport Harbor.

Taken from south of the layouts, the photo somewhat distorts the features of the course because of its angle but reveals enough of Ocean Links to confirm its greatness.

And there are also reproductions of the Paul Moschcowitz paintings commissioned by Tailer, showing various views of the course. A number of the renderings were reprinted in *Golf Illustrated* sometime in the early 1920s. How many Moschcowitz completed is unknown, but Macdonald-Raynor historian George Bahto has accounted for at least a dozen, including one that never appeared in the magazine.

Most of Moschcowitz's works show a tight view of a single green complex and often include actual players who matched their skills against the layout. The Tailers and Macdonald were

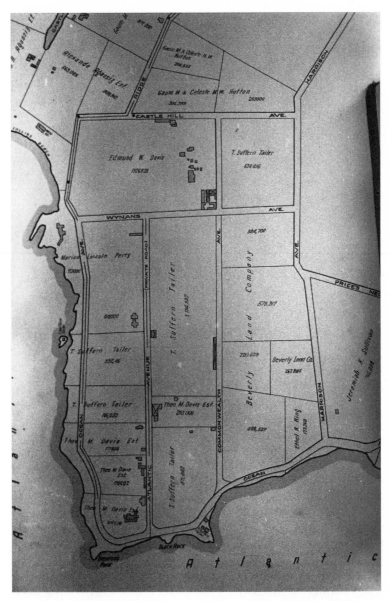

A drawing of Brenton Point from a 1920 Rhode Island atlas shows the area that would one day be Ocean Links (T. Suffern Tailer) and the second through eighth holes of Newport Country Club (Beverly Land Company.) (Courtesy of Newport Historical Society)

Even though T. S. "Tommy" Suffern Tailer Jr. grew up playing Ocean Links, he decided in 1931 to let the course go fallow after his father died, despite there being money in the will for the upkeep of Ocean Links. (Courtesy of Patrick Hayes Jr.)

subjects, as were Hayes and amateurs Francis Ouimet, Jess Sweetser, and Bobby Jones.

The *New York Times* heralded the creation of the course and the founding of the Golf Mashie Tournament with in-depth articles. The demise of the course was chronicled in far fewer words.

A scrapbook of newspaper and magazine clippings, along with original photos chronicling the history of Ocean Links, was compiled by Patrick Hayes, John's son, a fine golfer in his own right and frequent playing partner of Tailer Jr. The scrapbook preserves what precious little documented history is left of the course.

T. Suffern Tailer commissioned Paul Moschowitz to paint a series of views of Ocean Links and they all include people who had been on the layout. Here Eddie Driggs putts as Jess Sweetser waits, while Tailer and his son Tommy look on. (Courtesy of Patrick Hayes Jr.)

Finding bits and pieces of Ocean Links is not always that difficult. There is the aerial photo to go by as well as Bahto's drawing of the routing, working off the memory of Pat Hayes.

Together they form a veritable treasure map showing the way to parts of the fourth, fifth, sixth, and seventh holes, which are all are easily located on park property.

Much of what remains is buried, but sometimes the course reveals itself.

The left fairway bunker of what was the eighth hole was un-covered by Newport summer resident Dave Donatelli in 2003 during clearing of a vacant, overgrown parcel of land he owns. Donatelli had no knowledge of the course when he found the bunker, but in an eerie coincidence he had named his house Ocean Links shortly after purchasing it in 2000.

With even more effort—as well as waterlogged boots and torn clothing—other parts can be seen, including what remains of a famous symbol of the course, the Well of Fame, commissioned by Tailer to honor his champions.

Accomplished golfer Patrick Hayes holds his form in front of the Newport Country Club clubhouse circa 1930. Hayes grew up playing Newport and Ocean Links. His father, Jack Hayes, was the golf pro at Newport for over forty years. (Courtesy of Pat Hayes Jr.)

It was here that winners and record-holders of the Gold Mashie Tournament—an invitation-only amateur event featuring the country's best players—were honored on a bronze plaque. Jesse Guilford, Ouimet, and Sweetser among others took home the title over its six-year existence.

The Gold Mashie was presented to the winner, and a Silver Mashie was given for second. The Gold Ball and Silver Ball prizes were given out for the best thirty-six-hole and eighteen-hole scores.

The Well of Fame's July 1926 unveiling was covered by the *New York Times* and, according to the paper, had as much significance for the town of Newport as it did for golf. "Like ancient Greek and Roman cities, Newport now has a well of fame, the first in the country," the paper noted.

Glenna Collett of nearby Providence, the U.S. reigning women's amateur champion, had the honor of removing the covering that kept the well from view, unveiling the supposedly 1,100-year-old Italian well curb to which a unique bronze top had been affixed. John Russell Pope, the importer of the wellhead and designer of the plaque—and in later years of the Jefferson Memorial—and two assistants were in attendance at the dedication. Ouimet also was there.

The well was also utilitarian, serving as a drinking fountain. A gate in the nearby fence also allowed golfers playing Newport CC to drink the cool water that flowed from the fountain.

Pat Hayes Jr. said that his mother remembers being taken to the well as a child to enjoy what was considered the best water around, even though the well sits less than 200 yards from the Atlantic Ocean. Water still flows from the well today, but the wellhead and plaque are gone; a brick foundation is all that remains.

While the locals may have come for the water, the golfers came for the layout, which was conceived and built out of frustration by Tailer when his fellow members at Newport CC—one of the five founding clubs of the USGA—rejected his idea that the course needed to be upgraded to remain one of the elite layouts in the country. Tailer was disconcerted by Newport CC's eighteen-hole Donald Ross design, wedged into land that was once home to the original nine holes first laid out in 1892. In 1895 it became the site of the first officially recognized U.S.

The eight participants of the 1927 Gold Mashie Tournament, along with Ocean Links founder T. Suffern Tailer, standing to the right of winner Jess Sweetser. Francis Ouimet is second from the left and Tommy Tailer is second from right. (Courtesy of Patrick Hayes Jr.)

Open, won by Horace Rawlins, and the first U.S. Amateur, won by C. B. Macdonald.

Tailer correctly believed that Newport had been surpassed by Macdonald's newer designs, such as the National Golf Links of America and Shinnecock Hills Golf Club, as well as other courses such as Garden City Club and Myopia Hunt Club.

Inside the Tailer household, a different reason was given for building Ocean Links. Apparently Tailer told his son Tommy that he was building the course for him. Tommy was nine when the course opened. By the time he was fourteen, he was playing in the Gold Mashie, and by sixteen he had developed into one of the best players in the country. That year—1928—he became the youngest person ever to make the match-play portion of the U.S. Amateur.

It is believed that Tailer brought Macdonald and Raynor to first visit the Ocean Links site in 1919, and that work began that same year. By 1921 the course was open for play. There was not and would never be a clubhouse but a greenkeeper's building held one of the most valued collections of antique golf clubs in the country, most of which are now on display at the USGA museum in New Jersey.

The course was laid out on four disconnected parcels, some that Tailer had purchased as far back as 1911 and others bought specifically for the golf course shortly before construction began.

To have the course ready for the 1921 season, work continued through the winter as construction crews overseen by Rocco Nocco, Arthur T. Arnold, and William Edward kept "the earth loose at all times, dynamite being used in sufficient quantities and at timely intervals," according to a story in the *American Golfer*. Money was not an issue for Tailer, who came from a prominent New York banking family.

The course officially opened on July 9 "and was tried out by a group of experts," according to the *New York Times*. Included was a group from Long Island led by Macdonald and members of the Links Club, which he also designed. They came over to Newport via a "power yacht" and that night dined at Tailer's summer home, Honeysuckle Lodge, along with the president of Newport Country Club and the mayor of Newport.

With the opening of Ocean Links, Tailer's point was proven to the Newport CC and within three years architect A. W. Tillinghast created an entirely new Newport CC, junking the archaic Ross design and creating the spacious and stunning seaside layout that remains to this day, using additional land purchased across the road from the original holes, up against Ocean Links.

There is evidence, however, that Newport members may have gone to Raynor to have him build a new course, or at least take part in the construction. A 1923 receipt to Raynor from Newport CC shows a payment for $538.90. Whether it was for a consultation fee, plans, or actual work is not known.

Tailer did not just build a better golf course; he went a little further. On every tee there was a large white box, most likely used to hold divot sand. On each, in large letters, was the name of the hole. Since the nine were variations in design of existing holes, players received an education. For instance, the fifth was called "Ocean Drive Cape Hole, Lido." For his bunkers, instead of sand mined from the nearby shoreline, Tailer imported brilliant white crushed granite from South Carolina.

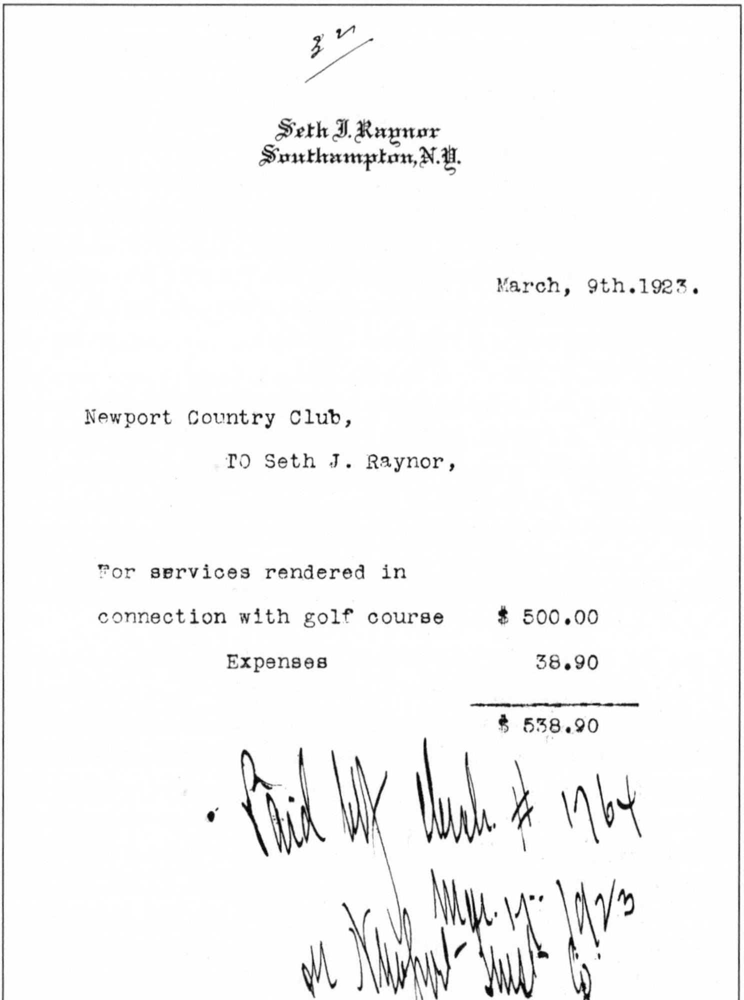

3/21

Seth J. Raynor
Southampton, N.Y.

March, 9th.1923.

Newport Country Club,

TO Seth J. Raynor,

For services rendered in connection with golf course	$ 500.00
Expenses	38.90
	$ 538.90

Paid with Check # 1764
Mar. 17 1923
on Newport Trust Co.

Seth Raynor at Newport Country Club? This receipt shows the club paid Raynor for unknown work, possibly a master plan. Members were impressed with his design of Ocean Links and may have turned to him before hiring A.W. Tillinghast. (Courtesy of Newport Country Club)

None of the boxes are known to exist and, in an odd twist, no sand remains in any of the unearthed bunkers, valued for more than snaring golf balls.

On the seventh tee stood a marble pillar upon which was a small bronze statue of a child putting. The shaft of the club acts as a sundial. It is exactly like the statue Pinehurst Resort has adopted as its official logo—referred to as Putterboy. Sculptor Lucy Currier Richards produced both. Richards was working from a drawing of a boy putting in early Pinehurst ads when she created the sculpture in 1912. The Ocean Links version now stands in the Newport CC clubhouse foyer.

The canvas on which Macdonald and Raynor created their first nine-hole course was hardly ideal. It was small, at about 70 acres, and the separate parcels forced a routing requiring multiple crossings of two lightly traveled roads. In one case, the tee and the green of the par-3 third were separated by Atlantic Avenue. Ocean Links played to a par of 36 and a bogey of 44, at a length of 3,034 yards.

The second problem was the topography—there was hardly any. Even though Macdonald and Raynor were not afraid to move earth to create a golf course, they preferred utilizing natural landforms to building them.

The two would do what was needed to make a golf course, as proven by three of their most audacious courses. Seven years of dredging—in part by Ringling Brothers circus animals—was required before the Country Club of Fairfield course in Connecticut could be built. At the Lido Club on Long Island, two million cubic yards of dirt were pumped out of Long Island Sound to make the layout. The two also spent $500,000 building a golf course for Yale University at a time when the average price of an eighteen-hole construction was $50,000. All three courses have suffered since construction. Lido is gone; Fairfield has undergone a series of unwise renovations; and Yale was altered by a misguided head greenkeeper.

Macdonald and Raynor had an approach to course design that was formulaic yet creative. Using what they believed to be the best hole concepts in the world—about twenty-five in all, with most of the originals found in the British Isles—the two would adapt the architecture to fit each course, in the process creating holes that involved the same strategies as the originals but were neither copies of the originals nor of any of their own variations.

Their work at Ocean Links held to those principles.

Interestingly, although Macdonald was involved with the design, he made sure that Raynor's indelible mark was visible, leaving no doubt it was a Raynor course. Two holes were adaptations of Raynor originals.

As was common with many architects of the time who realized players rarely had the chance to warm up before playing, Ocean Links opened with a relatively easy hole—a 310-yard, par 4 patterned after the fifth at Garden City Golf Club on Long Island, designed by Macdonald protégé Devereux Emmet.

On the second, Raynor mimicked himself, patterning the design after a hole on another of his layouts. Called Shoreacres, after the course where the original resided north of Chicago, it was a par 5 heavy in strategy. The Shoreacres version today looks much as it did when the course opened in 1922, giving a clear idea of the hole at Ocean Links.

It is peculiar, however, that the Ocean Links version of Shoreacres was in play a year before the original. Next came the par-3 Redan—with its tee shot across Atlantic Avenue—still the most copied hole strategy in course design.

The fourth highlights the problems the architects faced dealing with the site. First, not even halfway into the routing, the two were forced to come up with their second short par 4 in order to make the smallest of the four parcels work. They chose to emulate the opening hole at Macdonald's masterpiece, the National Golf Links of America on the eastern tip of Long Island. Like the original, the Ocean Links version bent right to left and enticed players to hit a bold tee ball over a series of bunkers down the left side of the fairway, amply rewarding those who pulled it off while at the same time offering a safe bailout route for the shorter hitter that resulted in a longer approach shot with a more difficult angle to the green. At National, though, the fairway drops off twenty feet from the tee to the landing area before rising up thirty feet to the wildly undulating blind green.

At Ocean Links the entire hole was built on flat ground, but the immense amount of strategy incorporated into the design makes up for the lack of ground movement. What remains of the green indicates that there was an abundance of movement, much like the first at National.

After a quick jaunt across Atlantic Avenue, players faced the third short par 4 of the round, a stunning adaptation of the Cape Hole that used more fairway hazards than any of the architects' other versions. The hazards were so large that they prevented a view of the green, and a bell was used to let oncoming players know they were free to hit. Almost the entire green can still be seen. Encompassing almost 12,000 square feet; it was almost entirely wrapped in a large bunker that sat well below the putting surface. As if that were not enough to deal with, the hole played dead into the prevailing summer wind with a green that sat fewer than 100 yards from the beach.

The next tee, which began a version of the Short Hole, also remains, as does a portion of the green.

It was next that Raynor and Macdonald created one of their most controversial and oddest holes ever, the 257-yard seventh, a version of Hill to Carry.

Macdonald says in his book *Scotland's Gift—Golf* that six thousand truckloads of soil were brought in to create a large mound that formed the Alps Hole, the top of which was about 185 yards off the tee. The Moschcowitz painting shows a mass of dirt that appears to be at least twenty-five feet high, topped with an uncomfortable double peak creating an extremely unnatural aiming slot, a feature Macdonald and Raynor thankfully never duplicated.

Whether the hill was ever modified is not known, but an undated black-and-white magazine photograph shows a twelve-foot-high hill. On the green side of the mound was a massive crossbunker. The green was heavily guarded by deep sand hazards. One golf writer of the day speculated that the hole would become the most maligned in the country. Whether or not the prediction came true, neither Raynor nor Macdonald repeated the mound design.

Next came an adaptation of the Road Hole, and finally Macdonald and Raynor made sure Ocean Links ended with flair by including one of only three versions of Raynor's Prize Dogleg ever built, a hole difficult enough to play to a par of four and a bogey of six, according to the scorecard.

At 460 yards, the hole required the boldest of players to hug the right side off the tee, skirting a large pine tree on the inside of the slight dogleg, and to negotiate a gamut of bunkering. On the famous Lido Club version of the hole, the few who dared go

This Paul Moschowitz painting depicts the seventh at Ocean Links and one of the oddest hazards ever designed by C. B. Macdonald and Seth Raynor. The hill, replete with an aiming slot, was situated about 180 yards out on the 250-yard hole. (Courtesy of Patrick Hayes Jr.)

for the green in two were required to carry a large sand hill and massive scrub just short of the putting surface. At Ocean Links, with no such features to intimidate golfers, Raynor rotated the green 90 degrees, creating a fishhook turn so that carrying a greenside bunker on the approach also meant hitting to a narrow putting surface, requiring the effort to be nothing less than perfect. Players opting to play the more conservative route and lay up left had a wider green to shoot at on their approach.

It seemed an impossible hole to par with 1920s ball and club technology, but George Von Elm proved otherwise during the 1928 Golden Mashie, turning in what was called one of the outstanding golf achievements of the year by the golfing press. He defeated his nearest competitors by an amazing 21 strokes, shooting rounds of 65-67-71-69–272, 16 under par and tying the lowest competitive 72-hole score ever. Incredibly, his eight rounds over the Prize Dogleg were played in 1 under par, ending with an exclamation point as his lone birdie came on his final hole of the tournament.

T. Suffern Tailer, second from left, and George Von Elm hold the Gold Mashie trophy. Von Elm won in 1928 with a score of 272, 21 shots better than second place. Tailer died in December of that year. As a result, the Gold Mashie was never played again. (Courtesy of Patrick Hayes Jr.)

Just like Ocean Links itself, though, Von Elm's achievement has all but disappeared, existing now as just a hazy memory or a fading yellow newspaper clipping tucked neatly into an album.

Tailer dropped dead at the Christmas dinner table of his in-laws in 1928. The following March, his wife, Harriet Brown Tailer, announced the cancellation of the Gold Mashie Tournament. That October, the *New York Times* covered the announcement by Tailer's wife of the abandonment of the course in two paragraphs that led off a lengthy report on the Newport social scene. "She regrets that the course can no longer serve the purpose for which her husband had established it. The land will be placed on the market," read the piece. "T. Suffern Tailer Jr., son of Mrs. Tailer, does not care to maintain these contests and prefers to play the Newport Country Club course." In the next paragraph, the paper reported on a luncheon given by Mrs. Henry Delafield Phelps.

It appears that putting an end to Ocean Links was Tommy Tailer's decision. Less than a week after the announcement of the course's demise, the *Times* reported that through his trust, the elder Tailer left more than $139,000 for the upkeep of Ocean Links, "and was predicated on the life of his son... or on his [the son's] election to discontinue retention of the property. This he last did."

The decision probably came about because Tommy's life had taken him away from Newport and he may have needed the money, according to surviving family members.

In the same year Tailer abandoned Ocean Links, he married at the age of nineteen and moved to Long Island, where he played his high level of golf at such illustrious courses as Piping Rock, The Creek, National, Shinnecock, and Deepdale—all Raynor or Macdonald designs. He had three daughters in the first five years of his marriage but was divorced by 1939.

He competed successfully in golf on the national and regional level until 1940, when he won the Metropolitan Open and the Long Island Open, and shot a 17-over-par 305 and finished tied for thirty-ninth at the Masters. That same year he was drafted and was assigned to the Army, never coming close to combat. Family lore says that he continued to play golf during a tour of duty that took him to Governor's Island. In October of 1940, he remarried and had two more daughters over the next five years.

When he returned to civilian life, Tailer's competitive golf was played exclusively at the club level. He kept his membership at Newport CC and won a number of tournaments there over the ensuing decades.

He died in 1984 at the age of seventy-one, with none of his five daughters having ever seen Ocean Links.

Even though Ocean Links is long gone, the impact of the decision by T. Suffern Tailer to build the nine-hole masterpiece, whether it was a gift for his son or a means of showing up Newport members, lives on in the stunning Tillinghast design at Newport CC—and also some five miles away at another course on Narragansett Bay.

During the construction of Ocean Links, Tailer helped a golfing crowd made up of locals—not summer residents who played at Newport CC—buy land in Middletown and secure Raynor as designer of their eighteen-hole course, known for a short time as Bay Links and ever since then as Wanumetonomy Country Club.

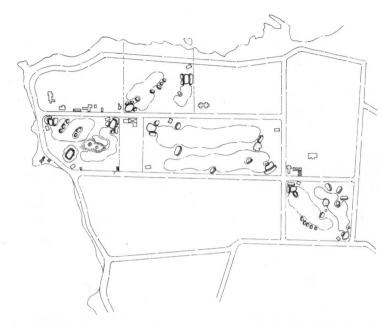

After looking over remnants of Ocean Links and viewing an aerial photograph, golf course architect Tim Gerrish produced this drawing in 2006 that shows how the Seth Raynor and Charles Blair Macdonald design might have looked. (Courtesy of Tim Gerrish)

It was at Wanumetonomy that Tiger Woods played one of his qualifying matches for the 1995 U.S. Amateur at Newport CC, where he won his second of three consecutive titles.

This would not be the last time Raynor and Macdonald would build two courses for one client. A few years later, while constructing eighteen holes for Yale University, Raynor was also contracted to build the nine-hole course at the Hotchkiss School, a private academy in the northwest corner of Connecticut.

It was at Hotchkiss that Raynor met Charles Banks, a teacher who was the school's liaison to the golf project. Banks would become so enamored with the field of golf course construction that he left teaching to join Raynor's firm, eventually overseeing the completion of more than thirty courses when Raynor died of pneumonia at the age of 52. Banks would also design more than thirty of his own works before he, too, died at an early age.

A good portion of the original Hotchkiss layout has been lost to the widening of town roads, the expansion of the campus, and ill-advised renovations, but what remains is at times phenomenal. The joy of putting the sixth green alone makes the journey worthwhile.

It appears Raynor did not devote as much time to Wanumetonomy as he did to more high-profile courses, but there are flashes of brilliance. The green of the Maiden Hole is one of boldest compositions Raynor created. The scope of the Eden Hole green is nothing short of stunning.

Both stand as some of Raynor's finest work and most assuredly offer a glimpse into the greatness that was once Ocean Links.

In Search of
Ocean Links

When I conceived the Ocean Links chapter of this book I had a simple plan: research and write about one of the greatest of the lost golf courses, which was cast off in 1931, ten years after the Charles Blair Macdonald–Seth Raynor design opened.

I had been informed that very little of the course remained, wiped away by the construction of high-priced houses and a state park. I thought I would have what I needed with a few visits to the property and a few stops at the Newport Historical Society. That is not how it worked out.

I've made over twenty visits to the course, multiple stops at the historical society, and even more to the law office of Patrick Hayes to see the family scrapbook filled with Ocean Links newspaper and magazine clippings and photos. I've spent nearly a hundred hours delving into *New York Times* computerized archives, and spent double that much time on the phone with Macdonald-Raynor historian George Bahto, my enabler with this addiction.

This search affected my job, my relationships, the expected life of my car, and my bank account. Thanks to my frequent stops at the Claiborne Pell Bridge toll plaza, the state of Rhode Island was able to give the mammoth structure a new coat of paint.

I've scared a number of park-goers as I stumbled out of bushes and thickets, appearing simultaneously ecstatic and confused, and bleeding from the scrapes inflicted by the thorns while I carried what must have looked like a medieval weapon but was actually just a soil probe. I always skipped the explanation, nodded, and moved on before someone called the police.

I've seen the frightened faces of complete strangers unfortunate enough to pull up a barstool next to mine as I rambled on about the Ocean Links ninth hole, a rare version of Raynor's Prize Dogleg.

I swear I've heard my friend talking about an intervention and wondering aloud whether there is a group that helps people like me.

"Hi, my name is Anthony and I have a golf course archeology problem."

I know when I became hooked: it was in the spring of 2002, after my very first visit to find Ocean Links.

I was visiting Newport Country Club, where architect Ron Forse was reconstructing bunkers in preparation for the 2006 U.S. Women's Open. He had a 1929 aerial photograph to guide his hand in restoring the work of A. W. Tillinghast. The photo also showed Ocean Links, and it was the only known aerial of that layout. I had read about Ocean Links in Bahto's illuminating biography of Macdonald, the man who along with his protégé Raynor designed and built Ocean Links for Newport millionaire T. Suffern Tailer.

With limited time and fading light, Forse and I decided to see what we could find amidst the tangle of vines, brush, and overgrowth. Within minutes we stumbled on a large mound of what we correctly believed to be part of the seventh hole. Later, in a corner of an open field, we spied what later proved to be the remains of the fourth green.

All I could think was how much more was out there waiting to be discovered. My gut instinct, forged over a fifteen-year career as a newspaper reporter, told me the story was much bigger than I first thought.

Although time and Mother Nature's relentless pursuit to retake what was once hers had obscured the remnants, more remained than anyone realized. Ironically, nature worked as both preserver and destroyer.

I found what I believe to be one fairway bunker and part of the green on the fourth hole; the tee, a fairway bunker, and the green of the fifth hole; part of the sixth tee; and maybe remnants of the sixth green.

The seventh hole was once defined by a man-made hill that we found the first day. This hill, according to Macdonald's book *Scotland's Gift—Golf* was constructed using six thousand truckloads of sand (most likely an exaggeration). The mound remains, with a notch carved into the top by decades of walkers who traversed the steep slopes, unaware of its historical significance in the golf world. The green and surrounding bunkers of the hole can also be seen.

Even when I didn't go looking I found residue from this once-great layout.

I was under the impression that the entire first, second, eighth, and ninth holes were gone, lost to the construction of homes in the 1990s.

However, in August of 2005, the president of Newport CC, Barclay Douglas, who proved to be invaluable to my search, informed me that a neighbor of Newport CC, Dave Donatelli, had discovered what was believed to be a bunker from Ocean Links.

I e-mailed Donatelli immediately, and we set up a meeting at his home in two days' time. I would have been at his door that very same night had he asked me.

What Donatelli uncovered was not just a fairway hazard from the eighth hole but also a veritable museum piece protected for nearly seventy years from golfers, mowers, and the elements by the same tangle of growth that had hidden it from view. With the care and tenderness of seasoned Egyptian archeologists, workmen peeled back flora and fauna to reveal a bunker so well preserved one can almost see the handprints of the original builders. No grass grew on the mounding; there was no sand on the floor. It looked as though Seth Raynor had signed off on the original work the day before.

Perhaps Donatelli was fated to own the property and discover the bunker.

A few months after moving into the summer house in 2000, Donatelli decided to keep to local tradition and name his home, unaware that his land was once part of a legendary golf course.

"I looked out this window and saw the ocean," he told me that August day, standing in the master bedroom and pointing to Narragansett Bay. Turning to his left he continued: "Then I looked over there and saw the country club, so I just named it Ocean Links."

Chills.

It's not just about driving and putting here in the Twilight Zone.

With the care of seasoned Egyptologists, workers from Sam Kinder and Brother, Inc., meticulously remove tangles of vines and brush that at once obscured and preserved the Ocean Links bunker on the property of Dave Donatelli. (Photograph by Dave Donatelli)

The bunker was a thunder crack out of the blue, but for me only the second biggest find... so far.

The prize discovery would be the Well of Fame.

Located just off what was the seventh tee on Ocean Links, and just off the fifth tee at Newport, the well was the symbol of Tailer's masterpiece. It was designed by famed architect John Russell Pope, who also designed the house that is now the USGA museum, and who would later go on to design the Jefferson Memorial. The natural spring had long been a favorite of the locals. When Tailer converted it into art, the 1926 unveiling was important not just to golfers but also to the town, as evidenced by the number of residents who attended and by the fact it was covered by the *New York Times* in story and photo.

According to the *Times*, "The members of the Summer colony were out en masse and there were hundreds of residents of the city present, as well as from many other cities."

Tailer imported what was believed to be a 1,100-year-old Italian carved stone well curb that was then topped with "a cover of bronze with a drinking fountain in the center." It also bore the

In 2004 while clearing brush on Dave Donatelli's land, workers stumbled upon a bunker in near pristine condition that once sat on the left side of the eighth fairway at Ocean Links. Donatelli preserved the artifact, regrassing it in 2005. (Photograph by Anthony Pioppi)

names of course record holders and the winners of the Gold Mashie, an invitation-only tournament hosted by Tailer featuring some of the best amateur players of the day.

The well was surrounded by crushed white stone and had what appear to be marble steps on two sides.

When the dedication was over, Francis Ouimet, who helped Tailer select the Gold Mashie field and had won the title in 1925, led the crowd in three cheers for the host.

A gate had been installed in the nearby fence so players at Newport CC could also enjoy a cool drink during their rounds.

The well, however, would host only three Gold Mashie awards ceremonies. Tailer died at the Christmas dinner table in 1928. His widow Harriet Brown Tailer announced the cancellation of the Gold Mashie early in March of 1929. That summer another plaque was added to the well honoring Tailer's memory, donated by many of the famous amateur players who had graced the course and participated in the Gold Mashie.

In October of 1931, Tailer announced the abandonment of her deceased husband's course. The land would eventually be

broken into smaller parcels and sold. No one knows what became of the wellhead or the plaques.

Over seventy-five years later, on a crisp, breezy, April morning, I waded into the brush in what was at least my third attempt to find the well. The window of opportunity to find a
vestige of the course opens in late fall when the leaves drop
away, but slams shut when buds turn to leaves in spring, reduc-
ing the view in many places to no more than ten feet.

The aerial photo does not have enough detail to show the
well and was useless for the quest. My only guide was a map
drawn up by Bahto for his Ocean Links chapter. He relied on
the memory of Patrick Hayes who was the only contemporary
of Thomas Suffern Tailer Jr.—Tommy to his friends—good
enough to hold his own with him on the golf course. Tailer quali-
fied for match play of the U.S. Amateur at sixteen.

Hayes's father was the longtime pro at Newport and was allowed to play Ocean Links, as were all the Newport members.
Patrick Hayes died before I met him but has played a key role
in my research thanks to a scrapbook he compiled, containing
hundreds of clippings of Ocean Links and Newport Country
Club.

I set out through the brush, following the paths cut by revel-
ers who party on the park property, and by streambeds carved
by the spring rains and snowmelt.

Walking in a perpetually bent-over position to avoid the low-
hanging branches, I attempted to keep the chain link fence bordering Newport CC in view as a reference point, but less than a
hundred yards into the trek I was convinced I was off track.

Squatting to get my bearings, I spotted a pale green stream
of tender, puffy watercress-like vegetation perhaps twenty feet
in length, standing out through the brush in striking contrast to
the grays and browns of the forest floor.

Perplexed, I headed in that direction and followed the plant
to its source—the Well of Fame, with icy, clear water trickling
out.

I was stunned.

All that remains is a brick foundation, but there was no doubt
that here was the well.

A large, gnarly tree fed by the spring arcs over the foundation,
concealing it from view. There were no signs anywhere of the
ancient wellhead, the bronze plaques, or the drinking fountain.

Patrick Hayes Jr. holds a family album of newspaper and magazine clippings compiled by his father and grandfather, including many that document the history of Ocean Links. (Photograph by Anthony Pioppi)

Still, I was ecstatic. I would have jumped up and down, but the low-hanging branches would have knocked me out. A quick two-step was out of the question due to the tangle of vines. Yelling for joy would have been futile and drowned out by the whipping ocean winds and the crashing waves. So I smiled in lone silence—for a long, long while.

I bent down and felt the water, peering as far as I could into the well—maybe three feet thanks to the shaft of sunlight that—as if ordered—found its way through the branches and illuminated the well.

It was then that I noticed my sentry, a kite painted to look like a ladybug, caught in branches overhead. Brenton Point is a popular kite-flying area, and this was not the first time that a kite ensnared by the dense growth marked an important find.

I bent down again, running my fingertips over the surface of the water, and listened, waited. I'm not sure for what, maybe the ghosts of T. Suffern Tailer, Charles Blair Macdonald, or Seth Raynor. They never came. Still, I had no desire to leave. I knew the Tailers had stood where I was, as did tournament winners like Francis Ouimet and Jess Sweetser. Bobby Jones played at Ocean Links, as did Glenna Collett, the Rhode Island native and six-time winner of the U.S. Women's Amateur who held the women's record at Ocean Links; all must have taken time from their rounds, quenching their thirst with the cool water.

The shiver that ran up and down my spine may have been from the frigid well water, or more likely from the sudden sense of history that washed over me.

It is not just the course I have uncovered during my search. Along the way I have also become immersed in the history of the Tailer family, especially T. Suffern Tailer, in an attempt to understand the ephemeral existence of Ocean Links and the man that created it.

Back then, the *New York Times* extensively covered the influential Newport society of which Tailer was part. Ocean Links received press from its opening in July of 1921 to its sudden demise in October of 1931.

The Tailers' social life also found its way into the pages, from the fundraisers they attended to the parties they hosted.

Conversations with Pat Hayes Jr. and Barclay Douglas gave tantalizing insight into the family.

In time, I talked to Jean Tailer, Tommy Tailer's third wife—he divorced his first and lost his second to cancer—and chatted with two of his five daughters, Fern Denney and Toni Smith, the latter a Presbyterian minister who lives no more than fifteen miles from me.

The family tried to recall what Tommy had told them about Ocean Links, never having seen it themselves. He died in 1984 at the age of seventy-one.

They told me the truth about the death of T. Suffern Tailer: he died of a heart attack at the Christmas dinner table of his father-in-law, in front of his two children and second wife.

The *Times* and *Newport Daily News* sanitized the story of his death, reporting that Tailer died after dinner. Apparently it was believed that the truth would sully his impeccable reputation.

Along the way, bits and pieces of information on T. Suffern Tailer revealed more and more about a man whom I have never seen smiling in a photo.

A photograph in the Hayes album shows Tailer on the green of what I believe to be the sixth hole, looking on with a rather perturbed expression as Jess Sweetser putts out.

But photos in a magazine show a much different scene. Holding the pin is Sweetser's wife, wearing high heels. Tailer's daughter Betty is also there, standing on the green in what appear to be golf shoes. Tommy Jr. and amateur Roland Mackenzie, who played in the Gold Mashie, watch Sweetser's shot, putters in hand.

What first looked like an unpleasant day on the course for Tailer surely must have been a relaxing round with friends and family, yet there was no smile.

John Winslow, who is now in his eighties, holds a priceless wealth of knowledge on Newport history dating back to pre-Revolutionary War days, and he has answered a small but nagging question: what was the large pin on Tailer's lapel in some of the Gold Mashie photos?

It turns out that it read: Ocean Links Official. Even though it was his tournament, played on his golf course with participants he selected, Tailer kept with the custom of the day by designating himself and others—including Winslow—as tournament officials with the large buttons.

It was also Winslow who recounted that Tailer suffered from a weak heart in his waning years, which prevented him from

T. Suffern Tailer, owner and founder of Ocean Links, watches as Jess Sweetser puts out during a practice round, most likely on the third green, a Redan par 3. The friendly Tailer was almost always photographed with a dour expression. (Courtesy of Patrick Hayes Jr.)

The Gold Mashie was one of the preeminent amateur events in American golf but there was also a lighthearted attitude. Mrs. Jess Sweetser (wearing heels), wife of the Gold Mashie participant, acts as flagkeeper during a friendly match prior to the event; Tommy Tailer, right. (Courtesy of Patrick Hayes Jr.)

walking the course during the Gold Mashie. He was still able to view play, though, chauffeured in his yellow limousine over the various roads that skirted Ocean Links.

I can picture Tailer, with his ubiquitous stoic expression, sitting in the back of the large yellow automobile parked on narrow Atlantic Avenue in 1928. He is watching George Von Elm's tee ball on the par-3 third sail toward a green that from that vantage point must have looked as though it were sitting on top of the harbor.

Getting to know Tailer as I have has produced an odd and unanticipated effect: I have come to respect, admire, and grieve for a man who died before either of my parents was born.

I couldn't help but smile after learning of his impetus for building the course, of how his son was included in the Golf Mashie field starting at the age of fourteen, and of how he so fell in love with Newport that he registered to vote there rather than in his home of New York City.

It made me genuinely sad when I first read the articles on his death, the ending of the tournament, and the closing of the course. My admiration for Tailer grew after I read the facts of his estate and saw that he had created a trust to provide an annuity for his chauffeur, along with two other trusts for Tailer's sister and a friend.

Tailer is buried at Island Cemetery, but I have not visited the grave, and won't until I'm satisfied I've recovered all I can of Ocean Links and its history.

Maybe then I'll go and tell him what I've found, and how much I wish he were here to answer my remaining questions— and then, more importantly, thank him for what he did for the game.

Maine

A Coastal Journey

Bob Labbance

The coast of Maine is unique in the United States. Once part of a massive mountain range that rose thousands of feet above the sea, the landform was etched and submerged by advancing glaciers during the Ice Age. Known to geologists as a drowned coastline, it was shaped by fracturing that allowed water to rush into lowlands, leaving the rocky promontories as the irregular and elevated shoreline.

Although the crow-flies distance between Kittery at the border of New Hampshire and Eastport on the border with Canada is only 225 miles, Maine actually measures 3,480 miles of tidally influenced shore. In addition to the endless finger-like peninsulas that project into the waters of the Atlantic Ocean, more than 3,000 rocky islands lie in the bays, estuaries, and coves.

These outcroppings have been home to native seafaring peoples for millennia, with curious Europeans poking through the marshes and headlands for the past four hundred years. As early as 1890, sporting visitors jammed flags into the ground and played golf along the cliffs, pastures, and beaches of the stunning coastline.

Today there are at least thirty courses with a glimpse of the salt water, and half of those are nine-hole tracks that offer sporting play in fabulous settings, some on islands only accessible by boat.

An avid player with a penchant for casual and quirky golf could spend a week trolling the coast and come away with vivid memories, an unmatched sense of well-being, and a strong desire to return for more.

These courses do not feature cookie-cutter holes with perfectly smooth greens and lush fairways. Rather, these coastal outposts are more an assemblage of one-of-a-kind links with browned-off fairgreens and tiny, convoluted putting surfaces; most lack fairway irrigation. In wet summers conditions will be lush; in those dry years there will be plenty of roll. A talented golfer should be able to score well in either case. Golfing bons vivants who believe golf can only be good if difficult may want to adjust their thinking and travel plans—either that or challenge these layouts with hickory clubs, the weapons of choice when they were all constructed. True golfers, even armed with modern technology, will revel in these historic golfing grounds.

Great Chebeague Golf Club is a perfect introduction to the island courses of Maine and their nine-hole experience. The ferry that leaves Cousins Island is small and runs a limited schedule, and without enough room to park at the dock an excursion must be carefully planned.

Stanley Weld, M.D., penned a 1962 book about the founding of Great Chebeague, tracing the genesis to a 1920 blueberry picking expedition by George Spalding and B. R. T. Collins. The men were prestigious residents of the Boston area who loved the island and feared its demise without outdoor entertainment to lure younger residents.

Armed with a hundred-foot-long clothesline and a dozen stakes to designate tees and greens, the men planned a six-hole layout, originally maintained by the cows on rented pastureland. The layout grew to nine holes shortly thereafter and supported an avid summer schedule for decades, including boating excursions for matches played against members of other island courses.

Though the layouts on Squirrel Island and Great Diamond Island have since disappeared, Great Chebeague plays on, much to the delight of the spirits of the long-gone founders.

Today, Chebeague retains its island charm, enhanced by the quaint hilltop clubhouse with views to Casco Bay. The longest hole is a 385-yard par 4; the total of all nine reaches 2,234 yards with a par of 33, but numerous bunkers, deep rough, and constant breezes provide plenty of vacation challenge.

The standout test has always been the 110-yard, par-3 seventh, a hole that commences at an artificial tee on the stone pier dock, forcing a carry over open water to return to the island-based putting surface.

The tee for the 110-yard, par-3 seventh at Great Chebeague is a synthetic mat on the ferry dock and many are tempted to take a shot right off the boat. At one time, there were a half dozen island courses off the coast of Maine; Chebeague is the only public layout that remains. (Copyright Bob Labbance/ Notown Communications Company)

A little farther up the coast and down one of America's most historic peninsulas is Wawenock Country Club of Bristol.

The Pemaquid peninsula was first settled in 1600, and by 1630 a stockade known as Shurt's Fort had been erected. Destroyed by the natives, it was replaced by the more substantial Fort William Henry in 1692, although the French burned that four years later. A reproduction of the fort draws visitors to the settlement's two hundred old cellar holes and ancient cemeteries today.

Just shy of the fort is the Wayne Stiles–designed Wawenock Country Club. Stiles and his partner John Van Kleek fashioned approximately seventy-five golf courses from Maine to Florida and west to St. Louis.

When their partnership dissolved in 1930, Stiles concentrated his efforts in Maine, planning courses at Bath, Brunswick, Boothbay, Wilton, Augusta, Portland, and elsewhere, eventually retiring to a cottage in Kennebunk.

Wawenock is classic minimalism, utilizing a broad, tilted open piece of sandy soil for a winding march down and out to the fifth hole and across and back up to the clubhouse. Two distinct sets of tees create vastly different tests on the front and back, with the two concluding holes leaving a lasting memory of good golf and a strong desire to head out again for another loop.

The eighth green is a classic Stiles offering. Set in an upslope—so the green's surface is hidden from view a mere 134 yards away at the tee box—the carry often fools players into taking less than enough club. That invites a visit to the cavernous tomb of a bunker at the right front, and without the necessary short game skill a player may exit this pit with ball in pocket.

The routing of the ninth hole bends gently right from tee to green, while the terrain falls off sharply left. Beckoning bunkers guard the elongated green's entrance, and with an inevitable side hill stance for your approach shot, par is a more than satisfying conclusion to the round.

Farther "Down East," the town of Castine occupies a promontory overlooking Upper Penobscot Bay. The town was once the site of the Revolutionary War–era Fort George and is still home to the sailors and scholars of the Maine Maritime Academy.

Willie Park Jr. was lured to the attractive outpost in 1921, and the nine-holer he installed remains largely untouched till this day. In fact, the only bunkers that were added to Castine

Castine Golf Club is the only Willie Park Jr. design left in northern New England. The hilltop sixth green must be attained from the fairway far below, but once reached affords a comely view of the town's harbor. (Copyright Bob Labbance/Notown Communications Company)

Golf Club have since been removed, and some believe this is the least-altered original Park design in New England.

Park was the master of subtlety, and players often finish his holes wondering why they failed to make par. The nuances of the greens and perfectly placed hazards contribute to this mystery.

The 170-yard, par-3 second is a perfect example. Miss the green slightly, and the large sand field front right will gather your ball, demanding a talented escape for par. All the holes at Castine look innocent enough, but shot-making acumen is the only way to deal with them.

The best vista from any coastal short circuit is found at the carefully hidden Blink Bonnie Golf Links in Sorrento. The summer residents who enjoy this playground have little interest in transient play, so if you stumble on the course please don't tell them we sent you.

Resting on an eastern-facing hillside, the casual loop looks out upon Frenchman Bay and the nearby peaks of Mount Desert Island—you won't find a better outlook from any Maine golfing ground.

Linger at the green on the downhill 270-yard, par-4 second to soak in the view; then muster your strength for the next hole, an uphill par 3 of 200 yards with a sentinel oak protecting the right side.

Many of the greens at Blink Bonnie still retain swaths of a silky velvet bentgrass native to New England, and although they putt slower than your home course, they exude a luxurious aura of days gone by when putts could be struck with authority.

The Causeway Club in Southwest Harbor is the sole short track on Mount Desert Island. Separated from the hubbub of the Bar Harbor side of the island by Somes Sound—the only true fjord on the Eastern seaboard, nearly slicing the island in two—this waterfront course is well worth your drive time.

Rippled fairways conclude at greens adjacent to the waters of Norwood Cove, and crossing the water itself is your task on one hole. Only two of the par 4s approach 400 yards in length, but the total distance of 2,304 yards is a sufficient match to the par of 33. It all seems fairly benign, until the wind howls across the open terrain and puts some teeth in this fine old friend.

Grindstone Neck Golf Course is the epitome of the Maine coastal experience. The rocky spit of land derived its name from a ship that went aground with a load of grindstones onboard. The club is located in Winter Harbor, a sleepy hamlet rediscovered by the wealthy Philadelphia crowd when they sought better ocean views from their cottages than Bar Harbor could provide.

Golf has been played there since 1891, and there is hardly a flat spot on the nine twisting fairways. Some say the course is the only one in America with ocean views on every hole; the second and third greens offer up the best outlooks, with open water backdrops immediately behind the carpets.

The 317-yard, par-4 third starts at the water, rises inland to the 90-degree left hand turn in the fairway, and falls back to a greensite on the waters of Deep Cove. Ancient spruce forests border the left side, where crack golfers may wander after a failed attempt at a shortcut to the short grass. Few players are successful in cutting the corner, and why bother? All you need is two well-placed mid-irons and you'll be putting for birdie anyway.

A final stop on the coast of Maine odyssey should be the St. Croix Country Club in Calais. The distinction of this bilingual

Legend has it that Grindstone Neck is the sole 9-hole course in America with an ocean view on every hole. The second green is hard on Frenchman Bay with views to Ironbound Island and the mountains of Acadia National Park in the distance. (Copyright Bob Labbance/Notown Communications Company)

club—founded in 1927 on the St. Croix River that separates Maine from New Brunswick, Canada—is obvious to geography buffs. St. Croix is the easternmost golf course in America. Grab the earliest starting time and you'll be the first golfer in the United States to bask in the morning light.

That makes the 125-yard, par-3 sixth hole the easternmost green in the land—and once you par it, like other golfing pilgrims, you'll be perusing the maps for the westernmost layout— perhaps a nine-holer—and other extreme points of the golfing compass.

Fenwick

Katharine Hepburn's Playground

Long before Katharine Hepburn conquered Hollywood and dated billionaire Howard Hughes, the athletic, lithe beauty graced the layout of Fenwick Golf Course, a nine-holer nestled in a tiny Connecticut shoreline borough—the wealthiest section of one of the Nutmeg State's wealthiest towns. Since the late 1800s politicians, industrialists, and entrepreneurs have summered on the point—known as Fenwick—that juts out into South Cove and Long Island Sound near the mouth of the Connecticut River.

The course is a throwback to another time, to a hundred years ago when nine holes were played in well under two hours, when getting outside in the salt-tainted air and enjoying the day was the goal and par did not much matter.

In her autobiography, *Me,* Hepburn described Fenwick's inhabitants, who included her family: "Everyone knew everyone. They—that is, most of them—came from Washington Street in Hartford. They were Brainards and Brainerds and Davises and Bulkeleys and Buckleys and Goodwins. They were very nice— very Republican—very Aetna Life Insurance."

They were also golfers. The game found a place among the residents by the mid-1890s, making Fenwick one of the earliest courses in the state.

In Newton Brainard's history of Fenwick, he wrote, "The first course was due largely to the efforts of Miss Minnie Houghton and Miss Lucy Brainard, who made the first flags themselves and I am sure secured the tomato cans for the holes."

The work of those two ladies was done in 1894. The current configuration dates back to 1896. The present-day sixth hole is one of the originals, making it among the longest continuously used greens in Connecticut.

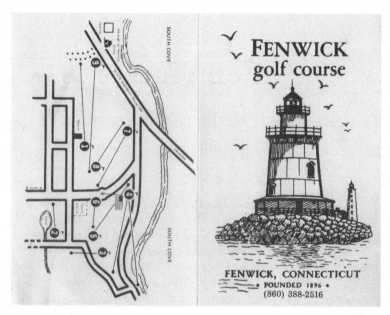

Located in the Borough of Fenwick, part of the town of Old Saybrook, this course dates back to the mid 1890s. The sixth green, once the ninth, is said to be the oldest continuously used green in Connecticut. Katharine Hepburn aced the hole in 1938.

A club of avid golfers was formally established in 1897, and soon after that the game had become popular among the guests of the long-gone Fenwick Hall hotel, a favorite summer destination that offered views of the Sound and Long Island.

The status of the golf course was cemented in 1900 with the founding of the Morgan Cup golf tournament, started by Dr. William D. Morgan, a first cousin of J. P. Morgan. Findlay Douglas, one of the finest players of the day, was a participant in the inaugural event, bringing it an air of legitimacy. He was in the midst of a stunning three-year run in the U.S. Amateur, winning once (1898) and twice finishing second (1899, 1900).

By the time a *Connecticut Magazine* writer visited Fenwick in 1907, the popularity of the new game had pushed other leisure activities aside, much to his surprise. "[T]o a large extent it has superceded bathing," among the hotel guests, he wrote. "When the followers of Neptune are becoming fickle it is an indication that golf is taking a strong hold on the young men and women in the country." The same *Connecticut Magazine* story also raved about the quality of the course: "Mr. Pemberton of London, who has frequently played there, says that the ground comes nearer to the great courses of England and Scotland than any he has seen in this country."

Hepburn's game was one of the best in the borough. She won her first trophy at Fenwick in 1923 at the age of sixteen, capturing the Approaching and Putting contest held just for lady members. She would repeat in 1924, and take the title again eighteen years later, in 1942. There was no contest from 1943 until 1948 because of World War II, but when it resumed, Hepburn won once more.

Undoubtedly her name would have appeared many more times on the trophy, but Hollywood called, although she spent as much time as she could in Fenwick.

Once, while she was playing Bel Aire Country Club in Los Angeles, Hughes showed the seriousness of his pursuit for the young movie star. She and her teacher were seven holes into a nine-hole playing lesson when Hughes landed his plane on the course, climbed out with his clubs, and asked if he could join the group. The plane had to be taken apart to be trucked off the property. The romance was in bloom.

Hughes also traversed the Fenwick layout, but undoubtedly his memories must have been unpleasant.

One of America's most famous couples shared a love for the game, but once they were on the course their goals were markedly different. One can almost imagine the svelte, smiling, red-haired Hepburn bouncing along, the dour Hughes lagging behind.

"I played for fun and exercise. Howard played always to improve his game," Hepburn wrote. "He was slow—he'd take practice strokes. I finally used to be almost a hole ahead of him. I was busy admiring the sky—the flowers—the relaxation. He would be utterly disgusted with me.

"'You could be a really fine golfer if you would only practice.' I used to think, 'And you could be fun if you weren't so slow.'

"So we drifted along. Misfits by tempo."

They were also probably misfits by skill level. Hughes announced his intention to be the best in the world, a goal he never approached. Hepburn's handicap was in the single digits. In two of her movies, *Pat and Mike* and *Bringing Up Baby,*

In this rare photo, a young Katharine Hepburn prepares to hit. Hepburn was a single-digit handicapper and a four-time winner of Fenwick's Ladies' Approaching and Putting Award. Her form can be seen in the movie *Pat and Mike*. (Courtesy of Ellsworth Grant)

Hepburn is called upon to golf and in the process displays her prowess. Her most famous scene comes in the first few minutes of *Pat and Mike,* as she shows up a loudmouthed playing partner by ripping off nine rapid-fire tee shots at a driving range. There is no deceptive photography needed. The first two swings and final are all shown from take-away to follow-through with one camera position.

Hepburn portrays Patricia Pemberton, an unknown amateur who makes it to the finals of the fictional Women's National

Match Play Championship, where she loses to the incomparable Babe Didrikson Zaharias—a rewrite of the original script, for Zaharias refused to take part in the movie if she lost in the finals as was originally planned. Along the way, Pemberton defeats other women professionals, such as Betty Hicks, a founding member of the WPGA—precursor to the LPGA—and winner of the 1941 U.S. Women's Amateur and Associated Press Female Athlete of the Year.

Watching *Pat and Mike,* which was filmed at Riviera Country Club in Los Angeles, it is easy to see that Hepburn is well schooled in the game. Her pre-shot routine is not one she picked up just for the movies, but through years of repetition.

Hepburn sets her feet, then stares out at a distant target. Next comes a series of waggles with the club head swaying over the top of the ball. For a split second the club comes to rest behind the golf ball before the take-away begins. Her setup is not ideal—she is bit too far from the ball, and as a result her swing is flat—but she makes solid contact firing at the golf ball.

In a scene shot on the first tee of the Hicks match, the camera set up behind the ball catches Hepburn's entire swing. She laces a drive that starts slightly left of her target line before fading back into the middle of the fairway as she holds her follow-through.

Spry and wisecracking at eighty-five, Hicks readily recalls Hepburn's swing.

"They didn't need a double for her in the movie," Hicks recounted.

She also remembers that Hepburn didn't seem too impressed with Zaharias, commenting once to Hicks, "She's rather outspoken, isn't she?"

Later in the movie, Hepburn hits a full wedge shot from a flowing creek by using her athletic ability to muscle out the partially wet ball; it checks up inside ten feet from the flagstick. There is no record of how many takes Hepburn needed to make the shot, but even so, the feat is remarkable. Her wood from a grove of trees late in the film is also impressive.

Although no movies of Hughes's golf swing have ever been made public, one blurry, out-of-focus photo of him playing at Fenwick shows a man who looks as if he has abandoned his stated goal of becoming the best golfer in the world. Hitting off a dirt road, Hughes, clad in a fedora, sweater, and long pants, was snapped just after impact. He looks off balance and awkward. Hepburn, ever stylish, is to the side, wearing a long-sleeved white turtleneck and black slacks, a small golf bag slung over her shoulder.

It was during a round at Fenwick that Hepburn's father had a memorable exchange with Hughes, foreshadowing the end of his daughter's romance with the philandering multimillionaire.

The first and only time Hughes came to Fenwick to visit Hepburn and meet her family, he made an awful impression. Among his transgressions: he spent too much time on the phone, spent hours reading in the bathroom, and objected loudly to the constant presence of Hepburn's ex-husband, Ludlow "Luddy" Ogden Smith. Even though the couple had divorced in Mexico years earlier, Luddy remained a family friend and was often found at the house, usually with movie or still camera in hand, capturing the Hepburns as they went about their day, which often included golf.

During that round at Fenwick, Hepburn's father, Dr. Thomas Norval Hepburn, had enough of Hughes's contempt for Luddy.

"Howard, Luddy has been taking pictures of all of us for many years before you joined us and he will be taking them long after you've left. He is part of the family. Go ahead. Drive. You need a seven iron."

An irate Hughes knocked his shot to six inches and made the putt for birdie.

"Not bad in a pinch," Katharine wrote. "Cool."

There were other memorable events on Fenwick for Hepburn. On September 21, 1938, while playing with one of her regular partners, Jack "Red" Hammond, in unusually fierce winds, she aced the par-3 ninth (now sixth) hole for her only career hole-in-one and even more remarkable score of even-par 31.

They followed their round with a swim in the Sound. Later in the afternoon, the two went for a second dip but were soon driven back to land because of the large waves. Unknown to them or anyone else—the U.S. Weather Bureau predicted that the storm would not make land—the massive Hurricane of '38 was bearing down on Long Island and the southern New England coast. Within hours the Hepburn house was destroyed, part of it smashed to bits, part of it sent adrift in the Sound.

Katharine Hepburn and Jack "Red" Hammond sit amidst the ruins of the Hepburn family's home destroyed by the Hurricane of '38. The day the storm hit, Hepburn aced the ninth hole and shot even par with Hammond as her playing partner. (Courtesy of Ellsworth Grant)

She spent the next day digging in their beach in an effort to retrieve the family silver.

The course has changed since Hepburn honed her game there, mostly for the better. In the 1940s it became a public course, owned by the borough. There is no pro shop, so green fees are paid at either the borough office next to the maintenance facility or the starter's shack. Some greens have been rebuilt, not all successfully. Bunkers were added while others, sadly, were taken away, but the original flavor has not been lost. Fenwick stands in rare company among American golf courses.

In the purest form of the definition, Fenwick is a links golf course. It sits on a sandy/gravel soil base left behind by the ancient ocean and remains not far from the sea. Although the hand of man has smoothed out many of Fenwick's undulations, there remain swales, hummocks, and hollows left behind by receding glaciers.

Maintenance practices help the links retain their style. Fairways are unirrigated and play firm and fast. The turf is anything but manicured. Grass species are numerous and include clover and dandelions, just like the links courses of the British Isles.

Almost immediately, golfers visiting for the first time know Fenwick is different. On the approach shot of the first hole, the most difficult par 4 of the layout, the nondenominational St. Mary's-by-the-Sea chapel comes into play if the tee ball drifts right. The small brown clapboard structure, replete with a bell tower, predates the course and is still used.

As they did in Hepburn's day, greens still range in size from small to tiny, and all but one are open in front, a must for a course with no fairway irrigation and a constant ocean breeze that swirls through the layout. In the fall when the leaves turn color, so do the myriad of grass varieties, producing a patchwork quilt of greens and purples.

Long gone are the wild blackberry bushes that once flourished throughout, creating natural hazards, but there is still plenty of old-time feel that makes Fenwick a joy to experience, not least of which is the walk that is required to negotiate the layout. The jaunt takes golfers through the heart of the borough, with at least four road and one driveway crossings required, offering nearly constant views of Long Island Sound, South Cove, and two lighthouses—Inner Light and Outer Light.

Locals own the only golf carts on the course.

The best walk is the only way to get from the first green to the second tee—a 300-yard stroll down quiet Agawam Road, often past residents tending to their flowerbeds or children chasing one another through spacious yards encircling grand summer homes, some in the Gothic style dating back to the 1880s. On the corner, in the shade of a large tree, is an ever-present golden retriever that revels in the attention lavished on it by golfers.

Off the nearby second tee, between a lagoon and the Sound, is the large Hepburn house, rebuilt after the hurricane. In 2003,

For much of her life Katharine Hepburn spent at least part of her summers at the family house in Fenwick, separated from the second green by a saltwater lagoon. The house was destroyed by the Hurricane of '38 and later rebuilt. Hepburn died there in 2003. (Photograph by Anthony Pioppi)

Katharine Hepburn died in the house. It was sold after her death and has been extensively renovated. The house sits watch over a par 3 with multiple tees that can play from 140 to 200 yards. Coming on the heels of the 420-yard first, it can make first-time players feel as if they have stumbled onto the most difficult nine-holer in the world, and that opinion does not change with the playing of the third, one of the toughest short par 3s in Connecticut. The three-tiered green surface of a little over 1,500 square feet is defended by sand left, chocolate-drop mounds right (unfortunately, a small pot bunker was removed in the last few years), and a twenty-foot cliff off the back. Depth perception adds to the adventure, for the backdrop of the hole is the far shore of South Cove, perhaps a quarter of a mile in the distance.

Par is always a fabulous score even at 157 yards, especially when the wind makes it play four clubs longer, as it does often.

And from there it is on to the knee-knocking fourth that for most of its existence was nothing more than a mundane par 4. But in the 1970s a back tee was added, turning the hole into a thrilling par 5 with a tee shot that requires a carry over a chunk of South Cove. The tiny tee box hangs out into the water, leaving barely enough room for two golfers at a time. One misstep and you could find yourself in the cove.

With a tail wind and a good drive the hole is reachable in two. A bad drive could end on the wrong side of Sequassen Avenue, possibly in the tangle of bushes, driftwood, and sea grass where the cove laps at the borough shore. It is an exhilarating shot reminiscent of the tee ball strategy popularized by Charles Blair Macdonald and Seth Raynor for their Cape holes.

The course finishes 4-3-4-4-5. The ninth is a spacious par 5, the fairway gliding down to a multi-tiered green inundated with subtle undulations. The last putts of the day could easily be the trickiest.

The green sits perhaps twenty yards from the starter shack, making it that much easier to pay for a second round and head back out for another nine.

Rolling Rock Club

A Donald Ross Stunner

"**H**ave you been to Rolling Rock?"
It is a phrase I have heard since the inception of the idea for this book; it was asked by golfers who had been there and by those who had just heard the stories of its greatness. Architects Brian Silva, who added nine wonderful holes to Rolling Rock Club in 1997, and Ron Forse, who lives an hour from the course and has visited it multiple times, trumpeted Rolling Rock to me soon after hearing of my plans for the book.

I was not steered wrong. The original nine at Rolling Rock must be mentioned along with Ocean Links, once in Newport, Rhode Island, and the original nine at Prairie Dunes Country Club in Hutchinson, Kansas, as the finest nine-hole courses ever in the United States.

In 1917, Donald Ross was on his way to becoming one of the preeminent and most prolific architects of the time, and when Richard Beatty Mellon came calling, he was by far the most prominent and wealthy client Ross had worked for. The nine-hole course Mellon wanted for his retreat in Ligonier, Pennsylvania, was the type of job that could propel the young Scottish-born designer to a new level, where clients would pay handsomely for sensational designs and spare no expense for construction in order to receive world-class golf courses.

Ross had only to look to contemporary Charles Blair Macdonald and his protégé, Seth Raynor, to see what those connections could mean. The two were designing almost exclusively for names like Vanderbilt, Rockefeller, and Morgan, thanks to Macdonald's ties to Wall Street and the world of high finance. While Ross was building nine holes in such places as Ionia, Michigan, Macdonald and Raynor were working in the

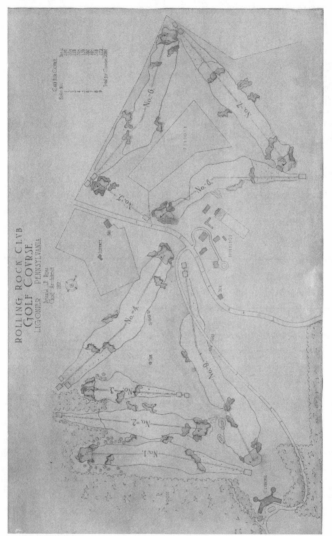

In 1917 architect Donald Ross designed a golf course that challenged players off the tee and on their approaches. Although built early in his career, the set of Ross greens stands with his very best—nine or eighteen holes. (Copyright Rolling Rock Club)

upscale summer colonies on Long Island and Connecticut's Gold Coast. To be fair, Ross was also employed as an architect for the Tufts family, which was in the midst of creating Pinehurst, one of America's finest resorts. But none of his clients—not even the Tuftses—were in Mellon's realm.

When he established the Rolling Rock Club in 1917, Mellon envisioned it as a retreat for family and friends from Pittsburgh, some fifty miles to the northwest of Ligonier. In the early days, Rolling Rock Club was foremost a shooting preserve, and to this day, golf remains just one of the activities in which members can partake. There is pheasant and duck hunting on the expansive property, skeet shooting, and angling for tiger trout in Rolling Rock Creek, which winds its way through the property. There also are myriad trails for horseback riding, as well as swimming and tennis. Golf was so far down on the list of priorities that in the early 1960s, when a number of members desired an eighteen-hole layout rather than an expansion of the existing course, Mellon leased the members land near Rolling Rock Club on which Dick Wilson built the eighteen-hole Laurel Valley Golf Club.

What Ross produced at Rolling Rock, though, rivals any eighteen-hole design of his. He used random and fairway cross-bunkering to an extent seen on very few of his other designs. The green sites are nothing short of spectacular, with undulations and movement that are suggestive of A. W. Tillinghast, Perry Maxwell, and Raynor. It is difficult to stand on seven of the greens at Rolling Rock (two through eight) and think that the same man who designed these swales, plateaus, and mounds became known as the master of subtlety. Ask Ross aficionados to name their favorite set of greens, and invariably you will hear about Wannamoisett Country Club in Rhode Island and Salem Country Club in Massachusetts. Nowhere on either of those courses will you see a single green that mirrors the best at Rolling Rock Club.

Although no club records reveal how often Ross was on site, his detailed plans that have survived show that the nine holes were built almost exactly as drawn by Ross associate J. B. McGovern. The course is broken into two parcels. Holes one through four and nine are on a knob situated off the back of the clubhouse, with the first tee and ninth green on one of the highest points of the property. Holes five through eight are across a

The ninth green, relatively tame compared to the previous seven, is framed by the clubhouse and Water Tower. The uphill par 5 calls for two exacting shots to leave an open approach to the flag. (Photograph by Anthony Pioppi)

lightly traveled road and make their way around a onetime paddock that is now the driving range. Ross must have been on site more than once in the three years during which the course was being constructed. It would have been to Ross's advantage to be in Ligonier often to make sure the project came off as planned so as to impress Mellon and others who would play. A rail line that ran through the Rolling Rock Farm property would have made getting to such an out-of-the-way location easier.

The course in its original incarnation opened on May 25, 1921, three years after construction began, but nary a word was written about the opening in the weekly *Ligonier Echo*. From the beginning the Rolling Rock Club went about its business in a quiet fashion, shunning publicity.

Ross designed a par 4 of 380 yards to begin the round, but those familiar with the Ross style of the time would immediately have known that they were in for something special. Rather than the wide-open tee shot found on most of his courses of the day, Rolling Rock had a triad of bunkers some 100 yards off that tee. Another bunker was in the right rough line 200 yards off the tee, and a cross-bunker on the left side of the fairway was 325 yards out. Carrying that last sand hazard would have been a must for those looking to bounce the ball onto the green using the natural contour of the hole.

At the 335-yard second, Ross announced that this was not just another golf course.

A large bunker, four feet deep, was positioned ten yards short of the green. An approach would have had to carry it to get at the putting surface, which features a series of wild rolls and pitches. The plans called for the bunker on the left of the green, with the putting surface on that side raised three feet, resulting in a mound that is more Tillinghast than Ross.

But Ross did not just design Rolling Rock, he also redesigned it—one of the few times he redid his own work during his prestigious career. The proposed alterations from plans dated 1947—the majority of which were never implemented—would have begun at the second hole, where he wanted to reduce the putting surface.

"Present green is too large for this type of hole," was typed onto the redesign plans. He wanted the right greenside bunker expanded into the putting surface.

He also may have believed the approach shot to be too easy. He called for filling in the left side of the cross-bunker, but he also called for a nasty little pot bunker some three feet deep to be added to the left front.

Throughout the '47 Ross plans are instructions for the reduction and elimination of a number of cross-bunkers and greenside bunkers, as well as the addition a number of pot bunkers—a style Ross rarely used—and the shrinking of the second green. The second, third, and sixth holes have separate, more detailed plans for changes in and around putting surfaces.

The reasons for the alterations are difficult to deduce. His abandonment of cross-bunkers, especially those at the beginnings of fairways, appears to have been motivated by acquiescence to the desires of high handicaps and short hitters, the only ones who would have to contend with those hazards. He also eliminated a few bunkers in the back of putting surfaces while at the same time making the approach to some greens more difficult.

In all, the '47 Ross plan called for the "closing" of thirteen bunkers (this does not include elimination of bunkers as part of the expansion of the sixth hole and rerouting of the seventh);

nine of these are fairway bunkers, the other four were behind greens. He reduced the size of two more, enlarged one, and added two pot bunkers. He also added one grass hollow and converted half of one bunker into a grass hollow.

While some courses abandoned bunkers during the World War II years to save on labor, that does not appear to have been the situation at Rolling Rock. In one case Ross called for the conversion of a bunker into a grass hollow, and gave specific instructions on where the sand from the hazard was to be used.

The only known aerial of Rolling Rock was taken in 1939, and it shows virtually every bunker from the original plans intact, eighteen years after the course opened. If the club followed any of Ross's suggestions, or did the work on its own, it was the conversion of fairway bunkers to grass hollows in some cases and the filling-in of other bunkers elsewhere. The club also eliminated all bunkers behind greens.

Ross's bold original design and subsequent proposed renovations continued on the third hole.

The first par 3 of the round is as difficult a one-shotter as he ever designed at 215 yards. Cross-bunkers originally sat at 110 and 150 yards, but the green is where the real trouble began.

The entire area tilts left to right. Ross wanted bunkers on each side to be dug down eighteen inches, with edges of the greens raised two feet and tapering off with a long grade. There was also a bunker behind the green.

The coup de grace is a two-foot-high undulation, thirty to forty feet wide and running through the green. There is not a flat putt on the green, and making up and down out of the bunkers is a virtual impossibility.

Hard as it might be to believe, Ross made the hole more difficult at the green in the 1947 plans. He removed the sand hazard behind, and then added another pot bunker in the right front that would be three feet, six inches deep.

Ross didn't let up on the slight dogleg left 395-yard fourth. Again, there were cross-bunkers at the start of a fairway that tilts to the left and is guarded on the inside of the turn by another sand pit. Players taking the safer route out to the right must then carry a large sand hazard sixty yards short of a green that falls off to the left. And in a touch more reminiscent of Macdonald and Raynor than of Ross's earlier work, he designed two tiers, one on the front right, the other back left. The origi-

At the fourth hole Architect Donald Ross encouraged players to flirt with a bunker in the left rough in order to have the safest route to the green. Choose to come in from the right and a bunker 20 yards short comes into play. (Photograph by Anthony Pioppi)

nal drawings called for greenside bunkers to the left, right, and back.

A perfect partner to the long par-3 third is the short, downhill fifth. At 130 yards, it plays as difficult as any short hole. Bunkers short, long, and to either side guard a green that appears to be tilted to the front left, but actually leans to the back left. A mound extending out from the left side bunker influences any putt on that side of the narrow green.

The sixth, a dogleg left at 392 yards and the first uphill hole of the round, rises some thirty feet, starting at about 225 yards. The green is two-tiered, with the back portion two-and-a-half feet higher than the front. In the 1947 renovation plan, Ross extended the hole by 132 yards, making it a par 5 of 524 yards.

It is paired with the most difficult hole on the course, and possibly one of the most difficult par 4s Ross ever devised. The tee shot of the 405-yard hole was downhill, with another two cross-bunkers in the first part of the fairway. The second shot, now as in 1921, is to a green elevated some forty feet. The approach is made more difficult by two bunkers, each over four

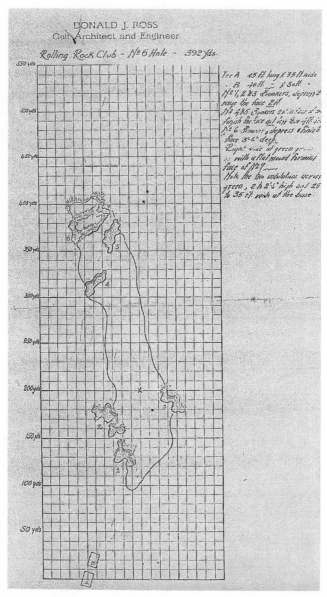

The 1917 drawing of the 392-yard sixth shows an uphill hole fraught with peril even in drive zone, not a common feature for Ross. The handwritten notes that accompany the plan detail the depth of individual bunkers as well as the green undulations. (Copyright Rolling Rock Club)

The most daunting shot at Rolling Rock is the uphill approach to the 400-yard seventh green. Players must hit a precise effort to the small green with so much movement any putt outside of three feet will have serious break to it. (Photograph by Anthony Pioppi)

feet deep, some fifty yards short of the putting surface, which is also guarded left and right by sand hazards.

The green is Ross's exclamation point, leaving no doubt that he intended for only two well-struck shots coupled with a deft putting stroke to result in a par or better. A two-foot-high knob in the front is teamed with a three-foot-high mound that extends from the left bunker face. On the right side Ross instructed the bunker to be two-and-a-half feet deep and "raise the face 2 feet with long easy grade."

Any ball that is more than ten feet from hole anywhere on the green can easily turn into a three-putt.

When he returned, Ross wanted to make the hole more ferocious. In the 1947 plan, he converted the seventh to a dogleg left of 420 yards.

Ross eases off slightly on the 345-yard eighth. There is plenty of room off the tee, but one of the smallest greens on the course is nearly ringed with sand, including a pot bunker at the rear, and although the putting surface is not as difficult as that of the previous hole, it contains enough movement to make all but the shortest putts interesting.

The ninth is the only par 5 of the original routing, and all of its 482 yards are uphill, with the green framed by the stately, two-story brick clubhouse. It is interesting that the putting surface has few of the features of the previous seven. It is relatively flat, slanting toward the left front.

In the 1947 plans, Ross calls for a significant change. "It would help if a depression were made into the front center lowering this section of the green from 1' at the rear of the depression to 1'6" at the front. This would leave a high level all along the sides and rear and the player could determine where the cup was located."

Ross made it easy to play again. The first tee is so close to the ninth green that superintendent John Yakubisin maintains it so the rear collar ties into the teeing ground.

It is a short walk and one that beckons loudly, even in such a serene and calming atmosphere. Nearly ninety years after it opened, the word "genius" can be heard echoing over Rolling Rock Club, perhaps the greatest nine holes ever built in the United States.

Sewanee

The Bishop Architect

The University of the South sits high above central Tennessee, perched atop the Columbia Plateau. For over 150 years it has been a bastion of liberal higher learning turning out over twenty Rhodes scholars. In 1983, Tennessee Williams, American playwright and a two-time Pulitzer Prize winner, left the university the rights to his body of work. A performing arts center on campus is named in his honor.

In the last years of the nineteenth century and into the next, Sewanee College, as it was called then, was best known for its phenomenal football team and for the astounding feat of the 1899 squad, which will never be equaled or surpassed, by any team, ever.

The Tigers were 12-0 on the year, outscoring opponents 322–10, and all of the 10 points they gave up were earned by a tough Auburn University squad that nevertheless fell 11–10.

What really sets Sewanee apart from any team before or since was an epic road trip that could not be imagined today.

Over the span of seven days, the Sewanee gridiron stars covered 2,500 miles, all by train, playing an amazing five times and not allowing a point. In order, the Tigers downed Texas (12–0), Texas A&M (10–0), Tulane (23–0), LSU (34–0), and Ole Miss (12–0).

It was the high point for one of the truly great college football teams of the era, but by 1915 the gridiron glory days were well behind Sewanee as schools with larger enrollments came to dominate the sport. There was the occasional victory over behemoths like Vanderbilt, but for the most part Sewanee was relegated to second-class status.

Yet by that same year, golf had established itself on Monteagle Mountain, and the school was on its way to a love affair with the game. Sewanee Golf Club has endured to the present day.

It appears that the efforts of one man, the Right Reverend Albion W. Knight, vice-chancellor and bishop at the Episcopalian school, lay behind golf's becoming less recreational and more of a serious sport on campus.

Knight came to the mountain in 1912 and stayed for fifteen years, until his departure to become bishop of Cuba. Before he left, he may have done something no other bishop will ever accomplish: he codesigned a golf course, much of which remains in existence today, complete with an array of short and long holes and a wonderful dash of quirkiness.

Along the way Sewanee became, in all likelihood, the first university in the United States to provide the opportunity of golf lessons for its students. The annual golf fee of $3 gave students membership to the course and the chance to hone their skills.

Prior to the first real course opening, the Sewanee campus, it seems, was already golf-crazy. In a 1970 newspaper story on the retirement of longtime course worker Preston Mooney, then sixty-five, Mooney recounted that even before sand greens were in place or cups were in the ground, student golfers used trees as their targets instead of holes.

Mooney, who was born in a house in the valley just below the course, began as caddie at Sewanee, making fifty cents a round, before moving up to the maintenance staff.

In 1915 the building of the layout was underway, with the efforts covered by the campus newspaper, the *Sewanee Purple*.

"The course was laid out by Bishop Knight and Mr. Eaton, who is very prominent in the literary world of America and who has considerable reputation as an amateur golf architect," read a small item in the sports section.

How Eaton earned that reputation as a designer is unknown. He had been editor of papers in Boston and New York, and had contributed to *American Magazine* as an art critic, all according to another story in the school paper that chronicled his visit to the campus in April of 1915 to deliver a speech. The front-page piece, however, did not mention his role in the course design.

The actual building of the course may have started in 1914, and went on until 1916 and possibly longer. It appears the intention at the time was to build eighteen holes, an idea that floated around for a number of years but never came to fruition.

The work was accomplished through the efforts of a variety of individuals and groups. The head of the engineering department and his "efficient corps of engineers" placed the tees and greens; the "forestry gang," as the paper called the student forestry corps, with three successive summers of "hard laboring" augmented by the work of a three-man full-time crew, succeeded in clearing brush and trees.

Even the football team lent its effort to the cause.

"Some thirty men who are preparing for the football season of 1915 under the leadership of Captain Dobbs are now at work for eight hours a day clearing the last nine holes and this fall the first nine which is now used for play, will be ploughed and sown with grass, especially imported for the purpose," noted the paper.

The condition of the layout was called "crude" by the paper when the course opened later that year, but the golfers were immediately enjoying the course even though they got unwanted attention from a roving gallery. As a result of the outside interference from onlookers there was a call for the formation of a golf club, but that would not happen for a few more years.

"It isn't much fun to slice a ball into the woods and have a half dozen natives follow in on the pretense of helping find it then cover it up for later reference for themselves," wrote a *Sewanee Purple* reporter, adding that "the galleries are very unappreciative and inconsiderate and always insist on getting all over the green when anyone is trying to cup the ball."

The paper regularly updated the goings-on and new improvements to the course. In the spring of 1916, $50 was needed to finish work but only $30 had been collected. Since land needed for expansion had yet to be cleared, there was congestion on a number of doubles greens.

The money was apparently found and the problem been rectified a month later, by which time only one green was being used for two holes. As the paper noted, this decreased the danger of players getting hit, "which adds to the enjoyment of the game."

The course must have improved markedly over the summer. In November the paper noted: "Every day sees more students and residents wending their way to the links for an afternoon of

wholesome pastime. Several amateur tournaments have been
played on the links since its 'making' began."

One of the avid participants in those events was Bishop
Knight, who consistently placed well.

The game was also given credit for medicinal effects upon
those afflicted with a jittery disposition: "It is a great aid to a
man in controlling himself ... He can also sit through a sermon
no matter how long or tiresome without squirming, wiggling ...
in any way or manner."

Apparently it became desirable to live along the golf course
as well. In June of 1917 owners of a new bungalow were looking to rent it out for the summer and placed an ad in the *Purple*
under the heading "Near the Golf Links." The price for three
months in the three-bedroom home that included a sleeping
porch, electric lights, and a telephone was $150.

During the fall semester that year the school firmly commit-
ted itself to the course and the betterment of the players, bringing Scottish professional Jack Cowan to work there and teach
golf to students. The hiring was announced in a small article
under the headline *Hoot, Mon!*

At the time Cowan was the head pro at Stockbridge (Massachusetts) Golf Club. He would be employed at Sewanee from
early November to May 1, then return to Stockbridge for the
summer.

Shortly after his arrival Cowan met with a number of Sewanee
golfers and was asked to list some of his accomplishments, which
he said included a 63 at the Ayr course and a tournament-record
69 at the Sterling course, both in Scotland. The exact courses
to which he was referring is unknown. He also held the
Stockbridge record of 68, six shots better than Francis Ouimet
was able to shoot.

Obviously in full command of his golfing clichés, and with an
eye on upgrading the layout, he told the gathering, "You have
the chance here at Sewanee of making one of the finest and
most beautiful golf links in America. It will take money and
time, but it can be done," adding, "Your third hole has one of
the most magnificent settings I have ever seen anywhere, and I
have played all over the world."

On the last point he may have been right. Trees and brush
had been cleared from the rim of the ridge, affording golfers a

In its earliest days the tees were also sand and guests were allowed on the course. In 1917 students, at what was then called Sewanee College, could join the course for an annual fee of $2; all others were charged $10. (Courtesy of Sewanee Golf Club)

stunning view of the surrounding valley that stretches for miles into Georgia.

In the early part of 1918 Cowan proved his mettle to the locals by shooting a course record of 65 in late February, then bested that in early March with a 31-31–62. Bishop Knight was in the foursome, and a story noted that "this score is only the more wonderful when the bad condition of the links and the darkness at the finish are considered."

It would be Cowan's last season at Sewanee. That summer he took the position of head golf professional at Oakley Club Course outside of Boston—the first design of Donald Ross—a post the school paper falsely lauded as "one of the three best positions a professional golfer can hold in this country."

Before he left Sewanee, the Scotsman came up with an improved design that would retain much of the existing routing, with only a small amount of additional clearing needed. Cowan's plan was not adopted until after he left. According to the paper the expected cost of the project was set at about $10,000, with the first $1,000 donated by an alumnus of the school "who is a lover of golf and spends his vacations on the Mountain."

For all intents and purposes, Cowan's routing is the one that remains today, including most of the tiny green sites that appear closer in size to irrigation heads than average putting surfaces. Finding one in regulation is made all the more difficult by the wind that rolls over the mountaintop.

The course is just less than 3,000 yards long, playing to a par of 36.

The holes are an interesting mix of birdie and bogey opportunities. For instance, Sewanee opens with a reachable 468-yard par 5, which is followed by the dastardly 406-yard second, the course's most difficult hole. Later, on the heels of the 278-yard, drivable fifth is the notorious 190-yard, uphill sixth, with a tee shot over water to an elevated green that drops off on the left and is guarded on the right by a large oak.

In the middle of the third hole is a piece of romantic history. Inside the former well house, where players once stopped for a drink of cool water, sits a stone marked "SH–ONT, 9-19-07."

At one time the rock sat on the shore of a nearby pond, and it was there on September 19, 1907, that Sewanee professor and avid golfer Oscar N. Torian proposed to his future wife, Sarah Hudson. He later had the stone moved to the well house, and the initials and dates carved into it.

Just like its predecessor, Cowan's course had sand greens; they were converted to grass in 1960. Preston Mooney was on the crew at the time of the change, as was his son, Dale Mooney, who like his father became a stalwart of Sewanee Golf Club as a player and a member of the course maintenance staff.

The younger Mooney began caddieing in 1946 at the age of eight and joined the maintenance staff in 1960, working until he retired in 2001.

Dale was involved with the relocation of the ninth green, extending the hole by about 50 yards to its current distance of 315 yards, the biggest change to the course in nearly fifty years.

He was also there when a dead tree next to the ninth tee was cut down and hundreds of small musket balls came tumbling out. Most likely the tree had been used for target practice by Confederate soldiers during the Civil War.

The sixth hole at Sewanee Golf Club may be the toughest. It is an uphill 190-yard tee shot to a tiny green. The large tree on the right encourages players to hit left, where a steep incline sends miss-hits careening into woods. (Photograph by Anthony Pioppi)

As a caddie he also witnessed back-to-back aces on the fourth (then a par 3) and fifth.

One of Mooney's most memorable moments came in 1951, while he was caddieing. He was part of a group on the second hole when a P-51 Mustang fighter stationed in Memphis crashed on the first fairway. Mooney said the pilot decided to buzz the course because he thought his brother was playing that day; actually he was at another course at the time of the mishap. Mooney said that a wing of the plane clipped a tree, sending it hurtling into the first fairway and partway through the fence of the tennis courts behind the first tee before coming to a stop. The only injury suffered by the pilot came as he climbed out of the destroyed fighter and cut his head on support wire for the fence.

Mooney has also created a little news of his own over the years. Even though a number of golfers who played the course, such as Lanny and Bobby Wadkins and Gibby Gilber, would go on to success on the PGA tour, Mooney holds the nine-hole

Sand greens were the way at Sewanee up until the 1960s. Here, players putt out on the first hole. Today's green sits in nearly the same location. (Courtesy of Sewanee Golf Club)

course record of 28, a feat he has accomplished so many times he has lost count. He's shot 59 for 18 "four or five times" and holds the competitive course record of 63. He considers 59 the competitive record. "We were playing for money," he notes.

He's also racked seven of his career nine aces at Sewanee, including one on the par-4 fifth hole.

At one point Mooney had been a plus-2 handicap, but when he and I teed it up in the summer of 2005, Mooney was a 1 handicap. The focus of round that day was not so much on our scores but more on his relating of Sewanee stories, which he did gladly.

A true gentleman with an easy Tennessee accent, Mooney barely stopped long enough to hit each shot, resuming the conversation with his golf ball still in flight. He rarely if ever went silent during his putting stroke, and along the way he showed me points of interest, told me course history, and pulled off some truly wonderful shots with a long fluid swing as smooth as warm apple butter.

He birdied the first hole and parred the rest, brushing aside my compliments after I tallied the score. He was more excited that we played in a little over 90 minutes than that he had shot 1-under.

A Mooney has been a constant part of the golf course since it opened. But Sewanee will soon undergo its biggest change since 1915.

Architect Brian Silva has been retained to upgrade the layout. His plans will retain and utilize seven of the existing hole corridors and reestablish long-lost views while adding a large practice area, all something that Bishop Knight would surely appreciate.

The Dunes Club

Apex of Modern Nines

Mike Keiser never intended on becoming a driving force in golf course construction. He just wanted to save his neighborhood near the shores of Lake Michigan.

Long before Keiser set out to turn a chunk of the Oregon coast into one of the world's great golf destinations, he built The Dunes Club, easily the finest nine-hole golf course built in the modern era (after 1959). It was an outright homage to one of his favorite layouts, the legendary Pine Valley Golf Club in New Jersey, with its large sandy waist areas, wide fairway corridors, and tricky greens. It was on his first visit to Pine Valley and Merion Golf Club that Keiser fell in love with course architecture.

So much did Keiser enjoy designing and building The Dunes that it spurred him on to his next project, Bandon Dunes, the three-course complex in Oregon that has become a golfing mecca.

Unlike Bandon, The Dunes is not open to everyone who has the money and desire to get there. It is a private course dedicated to golf, but unlike most other exclusive clubs—especially ones with less than a hundred members—it lacks all but the basic amenities players have come to expect. There is no state-of-the-art practice facility, no well-stocked bar offering an array of liquors, and no humidors brimming with fine cigars. The locker rooms are small, and there is not a bar or restaurant to be found—players and caddies alike can enjoy a soda or a coffee on the deck.

The location of The Dunes also fits that theme. Rather than being tucked among high-priced homes or hugging the Lake Michigan shoreline, it is situated off a residential neighborhood,

When Mike Keiser called upon the father-son architect team of Dick and Tim Nugent, he instructed them to construct a course modeled after Pine Valley Golf Club in New Jersey. They created the look using the natural sand dunes of the area. (Courtesy of Bukva Imaging Group)

with only one fleeting view of the water—and even that comes on the first hole.

An air of exclusivity does come from the fact that these may also be the most difficult nine holes to find in America.

The town of New Buffalo is situated in the southwest corner of Michigan, some ninety miles from Chicago, and right off of Interstate 94. Finding the course is another story.

A thick buffer of trees keeps the club hidden from the road, and nary a golf hole can be seen. There is no guardhouse or formal sign to point out the entrance; the only indicator is a small, numbered wooden sign fixed to a black chain-link fence. If you don't know the address, you'll never find the place.

The narrow driveway that affords just enough room for one car weaves its way around the trees and rocks until it arrives a quarter-mile later at a tiny, understated clubhouse.

In keeping with his bare-bones theme, Keiser passed on building a driving range. Players warm up by hitting off mats into nets (how municipal!) at two locations. The vast short game areas that seem to be required of any new course are not to be found either, but there are two large practice greens.

The unique flavor of The Dunes extends to the course and is noticeable as one steps onto the first tee.

Keiser sought to make nine holes that would constantly remain interesting to members. The layout features multiple and varied teeing grounds on each hole, and, in a twist unique to The Dunes, no formal tee markers are used except for tournaments.

A fan of match play and not an overly long hitter, Keiser's local rule has players deciding whether the winner or loser of the previous hole picks the next tee site. Since that can radically change the distance and the angle of play, the decision is no small matter.

The Dunes is very traditional in one sense—more than 90 percent of players walk, and those who do are required to take one of the club's skilled caddies. Not surprisingly, there is no uniform for the bag carriers, who dress in casual golf attire.

Keiser was just another self-made millionaire when he decided to build a golf course. His money was made from Recycled Paper Greetings, Inc., a company he cofounded with his college roommate in 1971 that manufactures greeting cards from recycled paper.

The area around the 60-acre course down the street from the Chicago native's summer home is reminiscent of the New Jersey Pine Barrens that is home to Pine Valley, replete with rolling sand dunes. "I bought the land to keep a townhouse developer from Peoria from defacing the area. It would have changed my neighborhood," Keiser said.

According to architect Tim Nugent, who designed the course along with his father Dick, Keiser first contacted Deerwood Country Club superintendent Paul Voykin about the project. Voykin is a proponent of using native grass species and plantings on golf courses. He directed Keiser to the Nugents, who along with Keiser traveled to Pine Valley Golf Club to visit the course and meet with then course superintendent Eb Steiniger to discuss his maintenance practices. Keiser spent days walking The Dunes property looking for natural green and tee sites, and he found many more than the nine he needed. The area had been mined for fill during the building of the nearby Red Arrow Highway, resulting in gouges and depressions that had softened over time and added to the character of the land. The work also

Golfers can play the versatile sixth hole from 135 to 185 yards with a tee that is wider than it is deep. The right side, nearly twenty feet higher than the left, doubles as the tee area for the eighth hole, a par 5. (Courtesy of Bukva Imaging Group)

caused a pond to form in the midst of the area. It was Dick Nugent who selected the nine best sites that worked within a cohesive routing.

In keeping with the Pine Valley motif, the fairway corridors are spacious, sometimes close to 90 yards wide. There is no thick rough; rather the manicured bentgrass is bordered by fescue areas, up to 20 yards wide, that meld into the tree line.

Again following the lead of Pine Valley, large sandy areas are located around greens, dotting landing areas, and bordering fairways. In their midst grow chunks of turf and natural vegetation—providing target golf on a grand scale. Only sand right next to green sites is raked and played as a hazard. The rest is considered a waste area; find your ball in a footprint, and a local rule dictates you must play it from there.

Once Keiser achieved his goal of building a standout nine holes, he was faced with the challenge of breaking down some negative preconceived notions about playing a nine-hole course. "If you quit after nine holes, you are a quitter," Keiser recalled hearing. He thought otherwise; as far as he was concerned, playing one round is quite acceptable.

Keiser also wanted to ensure that, for those who chose to play eighteen holes on a regular basis, the course would remain interesting day in and day out. He solved the problem first with the multiple tees on each hole, and then by having cups moved twice a day. "I did it to alleviate the boredom and tediousness," Keiser said.

The teeing areas are not in the long, flat, mundane runway style made famous by Robert Trent Jones, but are rather large tiered areas offering multiple angles for each hole. No hole has a wider array of options than the par-3 sixth, which the scorecard lists as having yardages from 135 to 185 yards. The 50-yard variation is only half the story. The tee is also wider than it is long, so that the hole presents an infinite range of possibilities, from short right to long left. The right side of the tee—which also doubles as the tee area for the eighth hole—is nearly twenty feet higher than the left side. There's no tedium or boredom to be found here.

Like many of the other greens, the sixth appears to be an island surrounded by trouble, quite a daunting target from the back of the tee.

Forced carries throughout the course are the rule. Only the ninth lacks any kind of waste area, with the green guarded in front by a lone pot bunker.

On the par-5, 534-yard third, how a player negotiates the trouble determines whether the green can be reached in two. The tee shot is usually a layup that calls for a left-to-right ball flight. Those successfully challenging the rough-covered mounds that mark the end of the fairway can take a crack at the putting surface with a mighty second shot. The second landing area is book-ended by the mounds and a waist area. Most players lay up with a mid-iron, then go for the green with a short iron.

A distinctive course should host a distinctive tournament, and The Dunes does—the annual Dunes Invitational. The thirty-man field, made up of club and mini-tour pros mostly from the southwest Michigan and Chicago areas, plays twenty-seven holes in one day. It is the payout, however, that makes the tournament different from all the rest. Besides the $3,000 check, winners

The fairways at the Dunes Club are generous in width but shots that make their way inside the tree line are sure to find trouble. The par-5 eighth ends at a small, elevated green. (Courtesy of Bukva Imaging Group)

also are granted a yearlong honorary membership to The Dunes and a week's stay with a friend at Bandon Dunes.

A number of tournament winners have gone on to the PGA Tour, including Lance Ten Broeck, David Ogrin—who holds the eighteen-hole Dunes record of 65—and David Sutherland. That's a distinctive set of winners worthy of such a distinctive course.

Prairie Dunes

Maxwell's Genius in Kansas

In the early days of 1937, work began on the first nine holes of Prairie Dunes Country Club. Less than six months later, on September 13, the course opened to great acclaim, and almost instantaneously Perry Maxwell's design vaulted into the rarefied air of America's greatest nines. At the time, perhaps only the Rolling Rock Club in Ligonier, Pennsylvania, was its equal. West of the Mississippi, no layout came close to matching what Maxwell had achieved amidst the sand dunes on the northeast side of Hutchinson, Kansas.

Legend has it that Maxwell thought the site to be the best he had ever seen—this from a man who had built Southern Hills Country Club a year earlier, and who in the year he built Prairie Dunes was remodeling Augusta National Golf Club, as he had done at Pine Valley Golf Club in 1933. If that legend is true, it is easy to understand. This area of Hutchinson is close in style to the land on which the great courses of the British Isles were built and which Maxwell had visited and studied years earlier.

When the wild winds whip off the plains and through the rolling grass-covered mounds, hummocks, and small hills, Prairie Dunes is more like classic British seaside courses such as Western Gailes Golf Club and Machrihanish Golf Club than any other American layout.

Perry Maxwell was a banker who became an artist and later went on to raise artists—one daughter went to the Sorbonne in France, and another studied photography in New York City. His first wife painted, and his second wife studied piano at the Julliard School of Music.

Maxwell talked of his work at Prairie Dunes as a painting, which is an apt description. To create such a pure golfing experience, little effort was needed beyond subtle brush strokes

performed by teams of horses with drag blades. This was neither sculpture nor carving. With the sandy soil, holes could be
massaged into the landscape or placed on top of the natural
features rather than gouged, bulldozed, or blasted into place.

His original nine (1–2, 6–10, 17–18 of the current routing)
are stylish golf holes that at times melt into the surrounding areas of nasty indigenous prairie grasses the locals call "gunsch."
Fairways rise and fall with the grace of a hawk riding warm air
currents over the vast Kansas plains, winding their way around
and past bunkers before gently transitioning into greens. The
undulations that add to the beauty also serve as stalwart defend-
ers of par. There are few level lies on the course, even in the
middle of fairways. In keeping with the practices of his contemporaries, Maxwell's course reveals the most versatile and talented
golfer by presenting myriad stances, lies, and shot requirements.

Greenside bunkers were so artfully placed that even the most
treacherous among them add to the beauty of the landscape
rather than interrupting it.

When brothers Emerson (June) Carey Jr. and William Carey,
heirs to the Carey salt empire, decided to build Prairie Dunes,
the two had seen many of the great courses of the British Isles.
William was a Rhodes Scholar and was twice visited by his father and brother while at Oxford University, and the avid golfers played some of the great U.K. links.

By the time the brothers had purchased the land that would
become Prairie Dunes, they had already been involved with
building a number of courses in the Hutchinson area. When it
was decided the salt wells under the Carey Lake Country Club
site needed to be mined, the brothers went in search of another
site, settling on a 300-acre parcel on the outskirts of town.

According to Howard F. Carey Jr., known as "Jake" and a
nephew of the Prairie Dunes founders, the land they selected
was inexpensive and so far out of town there was no direct road
to get there. Nobody ventured out that way because the rolling
land was considered good for neither cattle grazing nor farm-
ing; it would turn out to be ideal for golf.

Known as the Hutchinson Dune Tract, the land was formed
by wind-deposited sands from the Arkansas River at the end of
the Ice Age. In time a variety of grasses brought life to the
prairie. The dunes are now covered with such species as big
sandreed, big bluestem, switchgrass, and prairie cordgrass that

show themselves in hues of red, yellow, gray, lavender, and green. Thickets of woody shrubs such as the ubiquitous Sandhill Plum also thrive.

On Maxwell's initial visit to Hutchinson, the Carey brothers chauffeured him to the site. He asked to be left alone so he could walk and assess the property. With a sandwich and an apple as his only companions, Maxwell stepped out of the Carey automobile and into an architect's dream. He walked the property and beyond for the rest of the day, telling the brothers that evening the ideal site was a mile and a half further northeast on land they did not yet own.

He reportedly told them there were 118 natural golf holes in that part of the Sand Hills. "Now I just have to pick the best eighteen."

"He had a wonderful imagination. He would visualize the holes," remembers Jake Carey, who was twenty when the course opened.

Carey already loved golf and would go on to be Prairie Dunes and Hutchinson City champion. His Uncle June won the Kansas State amateur tournament in 1931 and would later serve as vice president of the USGA. Jake followed his lead, becoming a member of the USGA's Executive Committee as well as heading up the Public Links and Senior Amateur championships. He is a longtime member of Augusta National Golf Club, where he was a Masters official for more than twenty years.

Had it been left in its original incarnation, Prairie Dunes would now be considered the greatest U.S. nine. However, that was not to be. The Carey brothers made back their original investment by selling memberships, and eventually sold the club to the members who some twenty years after the first nine opened decided to add nine more.

Perry's son Press was the architect, some say working off an eighteen-hole plan his father had drawn up, but if that existed it has since been lost. Longtime Prairie Dunes golf pro Charles Craig testifies to having been shown the plans in the mid-1960s by then superintendent Everett Queen, when Craig was the assistant pro. Jake Carey, however, never saw the drawings and questions the legend.

Whether the plans existed, whether Press ever saw them, and whether he ever built the second nine to his father's specifications has never been determined. It is a fact, however, that the work of Press does not hold up to the original nine, plans or no plans. "Press did not have the imagination and vision his father had," Jake Carey said.

As proof he points to what he considers the ruination of the original eighth hole, now the seventeenth. In its first incarnation, it was a gut-check, 510-yard, dogleg right par 5, playing into the prevailing wind. The landing area was partially obscured by a large gunsch-covered dune on the right; a bold tee ball that skirted trouble would find the middle of the fairway.

"You bit off as much as you were man enough to bite off," Carey said, his disdain for the change evident in his tone.

He remembers the gunsch on the right side of the fairway being constantly matted down by the parade of golfers searching for their errant tee balls.

The fairway continued to flow right, then arced back left about a hundred yards from the green, leaving an ideal angle for the approach shot to a green elevated some fifteen feet.

In 1955, Press moved the tee from behind the current 10th green fifty yards left, creating nearly a dead straight hole and in the process entirely eliminating the strategy. The hole retains some of its teeth at the green, where one of the smallest and narrowest of the original putting surfaces awaits. On a windy, brisk spring day, I played the original nine in order with my friend Brett Zimmerman and Prairie Dunes golf course superintendent Stan George. Because of changes, it is impossible to re-create the original tee shot, but I was able to play from a sandy area that gave a hint of how the hole first played. The difference is astounding. Jake Carey remembers the old hole well.

"That was a sporty hole. Now it's a power hole," Carey said, the anger coming through in his words fifty years later. "I won't forgive them because of what they did."

A 1955 article from the *Hutchinson News* that ran during construction of the second nine had a drawing of the additional nine holes. The 17th was shown straight as a fencepost.

Press's shortcomings were also displayed in his original work, and nowhere more so than on the current fifth hole.

Carey said that the original plan called for the tee box to be well right of where it is now, creating a dogleg off the tee, but poor drainage prevented that. Carey scoffs at the design—even with drainage issues, something else, something more, needed

The tenth hole, originally the seventh, is the second of the two uphill par 3s. Playing at 160 yards, the opening to the green is on the left, opposite of the second hole. The bunker on the right is not as close to the green as it appears. (Photograph by Brett Zimmerman)

to be done. Now No. 5 stands as the least interesting and most uncomfortable of the holes, looking as if it were slapped down in haste, benched uncomfortably into a dune. The deficiencies become more glaring immediately as one steps onto the tee of No. 6, a short 4, originally the third hole and one of Perry Maxwell's best from the original course.

Sinewy, subtle, and at the same time dastardly, it tempts, invites, and teases; the entire test unfolding below the elevated tee for the golfer to assess and admire. A left fairway bunker is all but out of play, but one on the right side snares those shying away from the inside of the dogleg left. The green holds myriad swales and rolls, with the front of the putting surface pitched forward and at a deceptively sharp angle.

While's Perry's superior talent is evident on the sixth, it is at the fourth hole (eighth on the current routing) that his genius surfaces. Here, for the one and only time at Prairie Dunes, he decided to ascend the peaks rather than work between the dunes.

The third hole on the original layout—today it is the sixth—is a spectacular short par 4 that is not only stunning from the elevated tee box, but also demanding. An accurate tee shot and a precise approach to the undulating green are required. (Photograph by Brett Zimmerman)

The long par 4 sees the fairway rise sharply in the landing area. A well-struck tee shot invariably loses distance to the severe slope. The result is that players are faced with an uphill stance and most likely a hanging lie. The hole turns hard right for the approach; lying in wait is a wildly undulating green perched atop another dune.

The only respite Maxwell offers on the second shot is that it plays with the prevailing wind. However, any ball that falls short of the putting surface invariably rolls back down the face of hill, sometimes as much as forty yards.

Although Maxwell chose to challenge the dunes on that one hole, No. 8 feels neither forced nor abrupt, and it is considered by many the finest hole on the course. It has been selected as one of the best par 4s in the world.

The original nine played to a par of 35 and stood at 3,098 yards; the eighth (now the seventeenth) being the only par 5.

The original fourth hole—the seventh in the current routing—has been extended to a par 5.

While many of his contemporaries worked on the premise that an easy opening hole would benefit golfers, Maxwell's debut at Prairie Dunes is 403 yards, with the usual wind flowing from the left through the fairway.

The second is an uphill par 3 with a triad of bunkers guarding the front, and another at the back carved into the dune; from the tee the intimidating prairie grasses appear to encroach on the putting surface. During construction, workers who had cored out the green site used it to protect themselves against an oncoming tornado that eventually skirted the course.

The tenth hole is the other par 3 and like its sibling is elevated. However, whereas the second invites a right-to-left ball flight, the tenth calls for the opposite.

Maxwell's closing hole is a downhill par 4 of 340 yards, where bunkers right and a sharp drop off the left edge guard the narrow putting surface. It was here in 1962, during an exhibition with Jack Nicklaus, Prairie Dunes pro Ross Wilson, and Wichita Country Club pro Gene O'Brien, that Arnold Palmer drove into the right gunsch on his way to a double-bogey six for a 2-over 72.

If the subtle brilliance of Maxwell's design routing is lost on most players, the boldness of his greens is not. From the first hole to the last of the original nine, his large putting surfaces are rife with the wild ebbs and flows that made him famous, known as Maxwell's Rolls. They are coupled with nearly undetectable ripples, and together they can entice a seemingly well-struck putt to peel off its intended line and end up ten or more feet from the cup, an experience at once maddening and entertaining.

The devilish undulations that became his trademark remain, sadly, on only a few of his courses, Prairie Dunes being one. In most cases green committees more interested in high green speeds than in preserving genius architecture have removed his bold contours. So severe are the slopes at Prairie Dunes that superintendent George keeps them at a relatively mundane speed compared to those of most other high-profile courses—for dry prairie winds add even more roll over the course of a summer day.

George stuck to that procedure when the club hosted the 2002 U.S. Women's Open. Anything faster, he argued correctly, and the greens would become unplayable, embarrassing the tournament and the club.

The first hole at Prairie Dunes features a generous fairway, but architect Perry Maxwell did not go easy on the green. The putting surface is a dastardly mix of wild and subtle undulations that is sure to vex anyone who dares putt on it. (Photograph by Anthony Pioppi)

Maxwell learned well from his visit to the Old Course. Just as they are on many of the old greens, large portions of his putting surfaces at Prairie Dunes cannot be used for hole placements because of the severity of the slopes. Still, ample cupping areas are found on each.

The treachery of the greens is at its most severe when a putt has to travel from one "safe" section to another. For instance, while the middle right pin position on No. 1 can appear almost benign from within twelve feet, putting to the same location from the front or back of the green is a lesson in futility.

Even George, a single-digit handicap player who has spent countless hours observing, studying, and playing Maxwell's Rolls, is still flummoxed by them. Asked to read a ten-foot putt for a playing partner one crystalline summer day, George studied the line on the original eighth hole from a variety of angles, then threw up his hands. "How should I know? I've only been here twelve years," he exclaimed.

Midway

Down-Home Prairie Golf

Hundreds of sand green layouts dot the American plains, a phenomenon little known outside this region of the country. Of the nine states that have more regulation nine-hole courses than those of eighteen, only two, Maine and Alaska, are not in the Plains States.

Throughout places like Nebraska, the Dakotas, Montana, and Kansas, these nondescript layouts provide the only opportunity for much of the rural United States to tee it up.

The vast majority of these courses are played only by a handful of people who also act as superintendents and green committees, using nothing more than one set of gang mowers to perform their work on turf more commonly associated with backyards than fairways.

Take Route 61 north out of Hutchinson, Kansas, away from Prairie Dunes Country Club—the best course in the state—and you run into Inman some twelve miles or so down the way. A right onto County Road—also known as Highway No. 17—takes you through the tiny downtown and out into the wide-open country, and soon to Midway Golf Course, easily missed if it is not the object of your trip. The scorecard lists the location as "three miles south of Inman or three miles north of Buhler." From either direction, it's in the middle of nowhere.

The sign announcing the entrance is battered and peeling; it needed a paint job three years ago. My riding buddy, Brett Zimmerman, and I are here to experience sand greens first-hand, something that is impossible to do in our home state of Connecticut or, for that matter, just about anywhere else in New England.

Midway is the closest sand green course to Prairie Dunes—the venerable Perry Maxwell design—and the one to which head superintendent Stan George sends all those wishing to have the experience. Because of his recommendation, Midway over the years has played host to a number of high-ranking USGA officials who have come to Prairie Dunes. In 1995, after winning the U.S. Senior Amateur, Jim Stahl Jr. played a round at Midway.

For us it is a cool April day, and the sun that was supposed to send temperatures into the sixties has given way to a north wind that makes it feel thirty degrees colder. We pull into the dirt entrance and right up to the structures that signify the first tee—a small trash Dumpster and picnic table underneath a rain shelter, complete with a metal roof, no walls, and a sign announcing "No Spikes Worn in the Clubhouse." We are the only ones there, and are left to our own devices. A sign near the first tee gives all the instructions anyone needs: take a small envelope and tag from the box, insert $3 and the bottom half of the receipt into the envelope, and deposit through the small slot in the pay box, then attach the other half of the tag to your bag. For those thinking of avoiding the charge, it is not uncommon for members of the board of directors to stop in and check for tickets. Carved into the cement bridge on the first hole is a reminder to pay.

Inman resident Kris Lindenberger served as president of Midway for the 2005 season. He said that two groups dominate play: seniors who can't afford fees at other courses, and families where one or all are picking up the game. Daily green fees are $3; an annual membership is $40, and a family membership for husband, wife, and children under 18 is $50.

Lindenberger came to Midway in the early 1990s so that his son, who wanted to join the Inman High School golf team, could learn the game.

"I used to think golf was dumb," he said. "You think that's dumb? You should try caddieing for a fourteen-year-old who doesn't know how to play."

The elder Lindenberger became so enamored with golf that he bought himself a set of clubs and soon joined his son. He now plays with a regular group at area courses with grass greens, but still practices at Midway, although like many players he refrains from putting on the sand.

"It will ruin your stroke," he said.

The land for the course is in a trust owned by the Neufeldt family, which also owns the wheat fields that surround Midway.

At Midway there is no starter to fill you in on the local rules; the sign takes care of that. To pay, take an envelope and ticket out of the box on the right, slide the ticket stub and $3 into the envelope, and deposit the envelope in the slot below. (Photograph by Anthony Pioppi)

The nonprofit entity that runs the course employs one man to mow the grass. The board of directors provides occasional maintenance to the greens, such as pulling weeds.

Midway is an interesting layout that actually involves strategy, which is something not commonly found on pastureland courses. When he laid out the course in 1938, designer Jerry Jackson incorporated a small stream into the designs for eight of the holes; it functions at one time or another as a heroic, strategic, and penal hazard, sometimes coming into play with the tee shot and other times on the approach. The course measures 2,108 yards, with a par of 31. The longest hole is the 383-yard eighth, coming right after the shortest, the 133-yard seventh.

This day the greens are compacted and firm, with no indications that anyone has been on them for awhile. A coating of clean transmission oil is used to keep the sand packed tight; recent rains have also helped.

One way Midway tries to make miscreants cough up the $3 is to guilt them into paying. Every golfer confronts this message as they cross a ditch on the way to their tee balls on the first hole. (Photograph by Anthony Pioppi)

Because the greens early in the round are wet and packed, they do not need maintenance. But we go for it anyway; it's part of the experience. We take turns with the large metal rake at the back of each green, using the cylindrical side to smooth a path from our balls to the hole. Once we hole out, we flip the rake over, using the teeth side, pulling in a circular pattern beginning near the hole and working our way out to the edge.

Sand green cups are also different. Flags are permanently attached to a first cup that has a lip and fits into a second cup. The first cup and flag are removed during putting. The design prevents sand from accumulating inside the hole.

Since the greens are so small—some twenty feet in diameter—hitting them in regulation is almost impossible, so getting to a putting surface is usually accomplished with a pitch or chip. I'm zero for the round in GIR, while Brett finds two in regulation. No matter how well they are struck, there is no predicting where shots will head once they land; sometimes they

Brett Zimmerman performs his required service and rakes out the fifth green at Midway. We were the first group through that April day and had the course to ourselves, surrounded by the fertile fields of Central Kansas. (Photograph by Anthony Pioppi)

bound forward, other times they kick off to the side or just plain stop dead.

From there the real fun begins. Putting on sand greens, wet or dry, is surreal. A Stimpmeter reading would probably be two feet. For first-timers like ourselves, it takes nearly a dozen tries before we pull the putter back far enough and smash the ball firmly enough to get it to the hole. Early on it is not uncommon for us to leave fifteen-foot putts eight feet short. Even with a hard enough stroke, though, there is little indication of which direction the ball will go as it hops and bounds the entire way. Reading greens is a futile endeavor.

Midway is built on a table-flat piece of property with occasional groups of trees. One of our biggest problems is spotting the greens.

While every cup has a pin in it, each carries little more than a tattered remnant of a flag. Behind each green is a rusting metal pole and a numbered sign, most of them leaning at a decided angle.

Battered markers signify each teeing ground, mowed at the same height as the fairways. Finding a suitable spot to place our tees is futile in some instances, and instead we hit off clumps of turf.

The walking is easy, with no hills to climb or hazards to avoid, and it proves to be an enjoyable day and worth the trip. We just hope that our putting strokes can be revived in time for our next round on grass greens, the following day on the wild putting surfaces of Prairie Dunes.

Except for the occasional car or truck on Highway No. 17, we do not see a soul during our entire ninety-minute round. We play alongside massive fields, and I am mesmerized by the hundreds of acres of waist-high April wheat rippling in the steady north wind that brings a feeling of desolation. Out here on the vast Kansas plains, golf on a sand green course can be a lonely experience.

Wawona

Into Another Time

It would be so simple to say of the Wawona Hotel and accompanying golf course that to be there is to feel as if you've stepped back in time. This little nook on the southern tip of Yosemite National Forest is much more of a time-travel immersion than that.

From the two-story wooden hotel that dates back to 1879, with its wraparound porches and common showers and lavatories, to the understated rooms that come with neither television nor telephone, to its comfortable parlor, where nightly the tunes spanning the lifetime of the resort glide off the fingers and silvery tongue of pianist/vocalist Tom Bopp, this is America in the early 1900s.

Across the street, the Wawona Hotel Golf Course accentuates the feeling with its charming design that begins and ends in a meadow after meandering its way through dense forest and alongside rushing streams. Holes are bookended by small teeing grounds and greens, indicative of the time ninety years ago when golf was a leisurely activity enjoyed by all, for fun and exercise and perhaps, in this case, a break from viewing the waterfalls and mountains that drew tourists to Yosemite Valley in the first place.

Galen Clark first set up Clark Station in 1857, near the present-day Wawona Hotel in an area called "palahchun" by the local Indians, meaning "good place to stop." It sits four thousand feet above sea level, halfway between the foothills and Yosemite Valley, six miles from the famous Mariposa Grove of sequoias.

Later Henry Washburn took over the operation of what was by then known as Big Tree Station. Henry's three brothers soon joined him. Henry's wife Jean bestowed the name "Wawona,"

Since Wawona first opened little has changed, the course today looking much the way it did in this 1920 postcard. Nestled into the Wawona Valley at an elevation of 4,000 feet, it's the only golf course inside a U.S. national park. (Courtesy of Rick Lund)

meaning "Big Tree" in the dialect of the North Fork Mono tribe, upon the newly constructed hotel.

It was Henry's nephew Clarence Washburn who made the decision in the second decade of the 1900s to provide outdoor activities as an added enticement to vacationers.

As with many courses that began as almost an addendum to the accompanying resort—a swimming tank and a croquet court were added about the same time—much of the history has been forgotten or lost. For years it was incorrectly stated that Alister MacKenzie designed Wawona, the only course located inside a U.S. national park. Walter Fovargue, though, is responsible for the enjoyable layout.

On some holes Fovargue offered ample areas to drive the golf ball, while others require dart-like accuracy off the tee. Some greens are guarded in front, while others penalize only shots that stray to the sides or sail long.

Characters like Fovargue have faded from the golf world in the era of specialization. He was an accomplished player, teaching professional, architect, and multifaceted salesman.

He earned his reputation as a player by making the cut in the 1902 and 1903 U.S. Opens. Then, after a two-year absence, he made every cut from 1906 to 1916.

Included in that run was the 1913 Open, where Francis Ouimet captured the title and the heart of the golfing world at The Country Club in Brookline, Massachusetts. Fovargue shot a four-round total of 330, a mere twenty-six shots out of the legendary play-off with Ouimet, Harry Vardon, and Ted Ray.

His best finishes came in 1906 (at the Onwentsia Club) and 1916 (at the Minikahda Club) when he placed thirteenth each time.

As Fovargue was forging his reputation as a player, he was also establishing himself as one of the best teachers of the golf swing in the Chicago area while working as a professional at Skokie Country Club. A number of accomplished women were under his tutelage, including Georgianna Bishop, U.S Women's Amateur champion of 1904.

His popularity was strong enough that in 1910, he and George O'Neil, head professional of Beverly Country Club, opened an indoor golf practice facility in downtown Chicago that was immediately popular among area golfers seeking to keep their games sharp during the winter months.

In 1916, though, Fovargue made a major career change and set himself on a path that would lead him to Yosemite.

Walter Travis's magazine *The American Golfer* noted the move in its December 1916 issue, stating that Fovargue had left Skokie CC after ten years for San Francisco to represent St. Mungo Manufacturing Company on the Pacific Coast, "and also act as an understudy to Donald Ross, the eastern golf course architect. Fovargue spent several weeks this fall traveling with Ross inspecting courses and absorbing the latest ideas in course construction. He will superintend the making of the new course of the Santa Barbara Country Club."

The Ross/Fovargue relationship would most likely have begun at Skokie when Ross redesigned the Tom Bendelow layout from 1914 to 1915. Fovargue did the same at Santa Barbara, also a Bendelow layout that no longer exists.

His job with St. Mungo was nothing to scoff at. The company was the largest manufacturer of golf balls in the United Kingdom and was looking for a piece of the American market.

Fovargue may have stocked not only golf balls, but also other supplies such as scorecards. Letters from Clarence Washburn indicate that Fovargue may have been the course maintenance equipment salesman as well.

Fovargue's arrival at Wawona was mentioned in Clarence Washburn's diary, albeit briefly, though that brevity is no surprise. He noted an addition to his family this way: "Baby born."

According to Washburn, Fovargue first arrived at Wawona on August 2, 1917. The entry for the next day read, "Mr. Fovargue laying out golf course in meadow."

Two days later, Washburn wrote that Fovargue was finished laying out the course in the meadow and had apparently switched hats, taking on a role as teacher. "I had my first lesson in golf," Washburn continued. Three days after that, work on the golf course in "the field" commenced.

A September letter updated Fovargue on the exact number of each kind of tree—674 in all—removed from what would become the seventh fairway.

Fovargue was back in early March of 1918, and in April Washburn was writing to let Fovargue know that the men were maintaining the golf course and that the greens were fine, but that the fairways were getting long because "the mower has not reached Raymond yet." He also noted that Fovargue's recommendation for golf professional, Peter Hay of the Del Monte Club in Stockton, California, had agreed to take the job for the upcoming summer season. Hay and his wife would be a hit at the course. He would become pro at Pebble Beach Golf Links and later at Peter Hay Golf Course, also in Pebble Beach.

The diary noted that fairways were cut for the first time "with one unit of the mower" and then raked.

On May 21, Fovargue and Washburn's mother arrived on the same day. Earlier in the month, Fovargue had told Washburn that he needed to visit the course again to make sure the scorecards would be accurate. Washburn also noted that horse boots cost $14 for sets of four, and that each hoof needed to be measured for width and length, and that he would check on the status of the mower.

Hay, a native of St. Andrews, Scotland, arrived a week later and gave Washburn his first lesson the same day that "Mrs. Hay commenced working on the switchboard."

The winter and following spring were apparently kind to the Washburns, and the course opened in time for the summer tourist season.

On June 1, 1918, Washburn wrote to his friend George Uhl about the successful opening of the golf course: "Golf balls you sent arrived all OK. Started course off this morning and people playing over say it is in fine shape for play."

As the course was growing in, Washburn's game was improving. He noted this in his diary as well. In early July he played and lost three balls. Three days later he played again, shot 86 for nine, and lost two balls. The next week he shot 68, and two weeks after that it was a 56. The last golf entry came in August, when he noted that he had taken his second lesson.

It was not just Washburn's game that was improving—the course was improving as well. By the end of the year the layout was so good that Washburn was able to take a major step, ordering 150 sheep. "For the first time we have a whole golf course in which we can pasture them," he wrote to the farmer supplying the animals.

In 1919, the popularity of the course increased. A story in the August issue of *Pacific Golf and Motor* profiled the course in detail and covered an amateur tournament held over the Fourth of July holidays and hosted by pro Hay, "the untiring, good-natured professional. His rich Scottish accent and witty remarks created much merriment."

While Fovargue was working on Wawona, he was also one of four designers of the Lakeside Golf and Country Club course that was being built on what is now the Olympic Club in San Francisco.

With the inevitable entry of the United States into World War I looming, Fovargue made another major career move in what must have been an attempt to avoid combat, most likely giving up his job with St. Mungo, but continuing to design.

As *The American Golfer* wrote, "There is a general feeling among the professionals of the Middle West that those in the new draft age will be called on to enter some branch of war service. Walter Fovargue, who was located in Chicago for a number of years, and who subsequently became a ball manufacturer's agent at San Francisco, has entered the employ of a shipyard in Washington Territory."

GOLF

On the sporty mashie course on the Ahwahnee Grounds and on the NEWLY REBUILT WAWONA COURSE

YOSEMITE
NATIONAL PARK

Informal hospitality at Wawona Hotel

WIDE CHOICE OF ACCOMMODATIONS

Accommodations in Yosemite National Park throughout the year range from low-priced housekeeping outfits to the unexcelled comfort of The Ahwahnee, so that there is a complete choice of rates. During the golfing season, approximately May 1 to October 1, you may choose between The Ahwahnee, Camp Curry, Yosemite Lodge, Glacier Point Hotel, Big Trees Lodge and Wawona Hotel which is an ideal family resort—a splendid place for children—and adjacent to the Wawona golf course. In addition to golf, Wawona offers swimming, riding, fishing, tennis, camping trips. Since 1932, when the Wawona area was included in Yosemite National Park, Wawona Hotel has benefited by many improvements effected by the National Park Service in water supply, roads, trails, sanitation.

For further information address

YOSEMITE PARK AND CURRY CO.
YOSEMITE NATIONAL PARK · CALIFORNIA
SAN FRANCISCO · 39 GEARY STREET · EX BROOK 3706
LOS ANGELES · 540 W. 6th STREET · VA NDIKE 5022

NEW WAWONA GOLF COURSE IN YOSEMITE

Wawona Summer Resort

	Yards	Par
1	175	3
2	495	6
3	216	4
4	475	8
5	400	7
6	140	3
7	390	8
8	380	4
9	375	4
TOTALS	3,036	36

This pamphlet touts the Wawona course and the pitch-and-putt layout of the Ahwahnee Hotel, laid out by Robert Hunter Jr., who helped Chandler Egan remodel Pebble Beach Golf Links. Sadly, the course was bulldozed in the 1980s. (Courtesy of Rick Lund)

At that time, Fovargue also returned to the amateur ranks, but his game remained sharp. He won the 1917 Northwest Amateur as an amateur. In 1920 *The American Golfer* noted that "Walter Fovargue, the former professional, who has been reinstated as an amateur, recently set a record of 68 for the Grays Harbor Country Club of Aberdeen. His previous best mark was 70, made in a game with Mr. Heine Schmidt, former western amateur champion."

Fovargue had a slight edge on other golfers. While working in shipbuilding he also designed the Grays Harbor nine-hole layout.

After the war, Fovargue surfaced in Japan and, according to *The History of Golf Course Design,* made a significant contribution: "It was in the 1920s that the quality of golf architecture slowly began to improve. Hodgaya was the first modern Japanese design—it was carried out by Walter Fovargue." The course opened in 1921.

His final project may have been another Washington nine-holer, Willapa Harbor Golf Course, which dates to 1927.

His Wawona design, however, was falling from favor. In 1934, Clarence Washburn responded to a letter from Mr. and Mrs. John Smith, who had written to say they would not be back to the hotel unless changes were made to the course. "When you fix it so that we don't lose so many balls and when you have grass on the seventh fairway, we'll be back to play," they wrote.

Turf was so sparse on the seventh that the scorecard noted that players could tee up the ball anywhere on the hole.

Washburn invited them to return, writing, "Well we've done this and much more. Now it's a 1934 model course in every respect and I'm expecting all these golfers to return this year."

Apparently Wawona in its original incarnation was markedly tougher than the updated version, redesigned by Wawona's long-time professional, Harold Sampson, and Washburn. Ironically, Sampson had applied to design the original layout in 1917.

Fovargue possibly could have been designing for his own considerable skill level. For instance, the green of the downhill second that plays from 165 to 210 yards now has only a stream running behind the small putting surface. The first incarnation had "a small creek" protecting the front and left of the green, and behind "a grass mound and stream": quite the demanding hole, especially for 1918.

By the 1930s Wawona did not just attract vacationing golfers but also brought in some of the best club pros in California who made the trip to participate in tournaments that attracted a gallery. (Courtesy of Rick Lund)

Today the seventh is a dastardly 440 yards. Fovargue's design was 550 yards, with a more demanding tee shot than the updated version.

The tough finishing hole was somewhat subdued when, in 1932, the road separating the hotel from most of the golf course was widened to accommodate the increased motor traffic into the valley. As a result, the ninth green was relocated from near the pro shop across the road to an area adjacent to the ninth tee where it remains today. The original ninth serves as a putting green.

A number of bunkers were added during the renovation as well, becoming the first artificial hazards for Wawona.

The improvements seemed to rekindle interest in the course, as did a major marketing effort. Within the next few years, Wawona was hosting golf tournaments for amateurs and club pros from as far away as San Francisco, but the tournaments were as much about enjoying Yosemite as about playing golf.

The invitation for the 1936 Wawona Four-Man Team Championship pointed out that there were other activities besides golf at the hotel: "And all golfers who become disgusted with

their game early in the match, may have the choice of swimming, fishing, riding or taking the 15-minute drive to the Big
Trees—to reflect beneath the splendor of those trees, and to
wonder what happened to those well-meant iron shots."

Golfers today will be left wondering whether there is any
place better to enjoy the game.

Gleneagles

Wanted—True Golfers

The Phoenix Hotel sits on the edge of San Francisco's Tenderloin District, a rough-edged neighborhood where Vietnamese restaurants and no-frills drinking establishments abound.

The Phoenix is a rock-and-roll rest stop that caters to the myriad bands that come to play the clubs and halls, and to bask in the rich musical history of The City. The maids' carts are adorned with stickers of those groups—some famous, others hoping to be—that have played and stayed. Tour buses are omnipresent in the parking lot.

The building itself is a two-story U-shaped structure out of the 1950s, with a courtyard that contains what must be the only outdoor swimming pool in San Francisco's downtown.

I'm sitting on the bed in a large second-floor room of the Phoenix, with door open so the sounds and smells of the Tenderloin can waft over me. I'm trying to wrap my mind around Gleneagles Golf Course at McLaren Park when it hits me—rock and roll may be the answer.

Gleneagles is much like a three-chord garage band song—just about anyone with a modicum of skill can play it, but not everyone who tries has what it takes to play it right.

Gleneagles is not a charming stroll over tree-lined fairways or a sporty test of golf; Gleneagles is a love-it-or-don't-let-the-door-hit-you-in-the-shagbag-on-the-way-out kind of place, an inexpensive daily-fee municipal that is all about golf, not fancy shirts and expensive cigars.

This is a course that appeals only to a small percentage of players: those who would much rather walk than ride, who enjoy the shot-by-shot test, who care nothing about the whiteness of sand in bunkers or flower plantings around a tee box.

Cypress and oaks line the fairways of Gleneagles, but there is ample room off the tee. The sixth hole is a par 5 that is played at either 501 or 577 yards and can be reached in two from the forward tees. (Courtesy of Gleneagles Golf Course)

It is a municipal layout owned by the city of San Francisco and run by a concessionaire, and technically it's open to anyone, though in truth it's not. Gleneagles is for neither the faint of heart nor the recreational golfer. If leisurely three-hour, nine-hole rounds are your bag, if you think fixing ball marks and divots is best left to the grounds crew, if idyllic conditions are a must, skip Gleneagles.

If, however, you are looking for as demanding a nine holes as can be found in the United States, where rounds of under two hours are expected, as is repairing any damage to the course whether inflicted by you or someone else, then Gleneagles is the place for you. There are only two sets of tees, blue for the front, gold for the back—no men's, women's, seniors', or championship tees.

Carved into a hillside with nearly ninety feet of elevation change, flush against a housing project and buffeted by the same wind coming off the San Bruno Mountains that for nearly forty years made Candlestick Park an outfielder's nightmare, Gleneagles is a full frontal assault, from the opening tee ball down the tight first fairway to the final putt on the taxing two-tiered ninth green.

In an indication of its difficulty, 2004 Northern California Golf Association Public Links Champion Gary Young honed his skills at Gleneagles, where he was also club champion.

There is not an abundance of amenities to be found at Gleneagles. There's no official logo, nor hats and shirts bearing the club name. Hell, there isn't even a pro shop. Golfers pay green fees in the lounge/snack bar, called Old Peculiar's. Want a hot dog? Take it out of the refrigerator and warm it in the microwave yourself. The same bar offers a ridiculously wide array of Scotch, poured in generous portions at prices far lower than those at the trendy San Francisco watering holes.

The Scotch and the green fees are inexpensive. The attitude is free.

Before I headed out for my first round at Gleneagles, general manager Bill Smith was kind enough to give me one quick pointer as we stood near the first tee with a view of the San Francisco Bay and Candlestick Point spread before us.

"All putts break towards the Cow Palace," he said, indicating the venerable arena in the distance, "except those that don't."

Thanks, Bill, let me write that down.

My second bit of advice came from one of my three playing partners, Joanne, who told me in a voice sounding like it had inhaled a lifetime of unfiltered Pall Malls, "The only level lies on the golf course are on the cart paths."

She's not kidding. *San Francisco Chronicle* columnist Art Rosenbaum described the course, then called McLaren Park, this way after its grand opening in 1962: "It is not true that the par players at McLaren will need a mercury-bubble level, an anemometer, an altimeter, and one leg shorter than the other, though these might lend aid and birdies to the situation."

When I met Joanne, she and two longtime playing partners, Charlie and Bernie, were waiting to start their second nine. They have played together for years and, as usual, had a little money bet on the outcome. Unlike many of the games at Gleneagles, this one was more about the fun than the quarters that would invariably change hands when the round concluded.

The second green at Gleneagles offers a view of the San Bruno Mountains, San Francisco Bay, and Candlestick Point. Ground was broken for Gleneagles Golf Course and Candlestick Park on the same day. (Courtesy of Gleneagles Golf Course)

A few minutes later, as we stood in the middle of the first fairway, I had my initial taste of what makes Gleneagles, well, Gleneagles.

Bernie was mumbling about the pace of play of the foursome in front of us when he noticed that the two longtime Gleneagles players in the group were on the second tee while the two newcomers they were paired with were still putting out. Merely one hole into the round, and the regulars had had enough of the unacceptable pace and took matters into their own hands. At Gleneagles, slow play is an unforgivable transgression.

The two stragglers didn't get the hint, continuing to dawdle on the green until Bernie hit his boiling point in the middle of the fairway.

"Hurry up! Let's go!" he bellowed with an aggravated tone, whistling and waving his arms from a hundred yards out.

Bernie turned to me, his face red, rage working its way to the surface. "This is not a place to learn!" he huffed.

They finally moved to the next hole, but by the time the unfortunate twosome found their tee shots, less than a hundred yards away and buried in deep rough, our group was already waiting to hit, Bernie staring them down, arms folded across his chest.

"We're playing through," he shouted. Telling them, not asking them.

And we did, leaving them behind in a matter of minutes.

"And I'm one of the calmer ones," he told me a few minutes later, his blood pressure returning to normal. The others in the group nodded in agreement.

Although the attitude may come across as condescending and arrogant, it is neither. Gleneagles regulars pride themselves in playing quickly and courteously. Gaining acceptance with the regulars has to do with etiquette, not playing ability.

Joanne's Gleneagles handicap is in the mid-20s, Charlie's is 20, and Bernie's 11.

Joanne's well-struck approach to the second shatters the turf, leaving no divot, but she kicks in the gouge with the skill of a touring pro.

Leaving the course in better condition than you found it is a must at Gleneagles, because playing the ball down is the standard.

Can there be another municipal golf course in the United States that hosts as many rounds as Gleneagles—35,000—with so few ball marks on the greens or unrepaired divots in the fairways?

"We don't need rangers out here," longtime GM Smith tells me. "Every regular is a ranger."

Gleneagles is no men's haven, either. Although the vast majority of players are male, women are welcomed.

Joanne said she was given some words of advice when she first came to the course with a female friend in the early 1990s.

"'You'll do fine as long as you don't piss the boys off,'" she recalled being told, cackling at the memory.

Throughout our round she refers to her male counterparts as "boys."

All she had to do to placate them was to play quickly and mark her ball once on the green. By following those two simple rules, she became as accepted as any golfer with a Y chromosome.

Two holes into my maiden round at Gleneagles, though, my acceptance was still up in the air after I carded a pair of unimpressive bogeys. On the third I uncorked a beauty on the down-hill, dogleg-right par 4 that came to rest after 280 yards, just inside the 100-yard marker.

"Nice drive," Joanne said sincerely as I got to my ball.

"Now do something with it," Bernie added in a tone that bore no sarcasm.

The message was clear: at Gleneagles, one shot does not make a hole.

I hit my approach to fifteen feet and tapped in for par. The three gave me my due on the way to the fourth. Charlie told me that at Gleneagles, a par on any hole is considered a good score. I nodded and thanked him. I felt better about my standing.

By the time we finished the round, the wind came up, making a par on any hole a great score.

If Jack Fleming were still alive, he surely would've been smiling. The longtime construction superintendent for renowned architect Alister MacKenzie (and then San Francisco's superintendent for golf course maintenance) designed Gleneagles, then known as McLaren Park Golf Course, battling the local government as much as the elevation change as he went.

While with MacKenzie, Fleming worked on such notable designs as Cypress Point and The Valley Club at Montecito before joining the San Francisco Parks Department, for which he designed other courses, including the Fleming Nine at Harding Park Golf Course.

If Fleming loved Gleneagles, the powers that be in San Francisco did not. From the outset, McLaren received second-class treatment from the city.

Lou Nolan was a longtime heavy equipment operator for the city, helping build not only McLaren but Candlestick Park as well. He remembers the frustration of Fleming—who often ran equipment—when men and machinery were removed from McLaren in the midst of construction and sent to other city jobs such as the building of a neighborhood park.

Fleming had submitted a plan for eighteen holes in which the back nine would take advantage of a ridge that sits above Gleneagles and affords a spectacular view of the ocean and mountains. He was rejected outright by "downtown," as Nolan repeatedly refers to City Hall. A seldom-used park occupies the site.

The fairway of the third hole invites players to hit to the right side away from the trees—not easy as it is cantered toward trouble and subject to unpredictable winds. When the course opened, this hole came with an alternate green. (Courtesy of Gleneagles Golf Course)

Known as a micromanager by some, Fleming nevertheless is remembered fondly by Nolan more than forty years later. Nolan easily recalls his near daily instructions from Fleming.

"He would say to me, 'Louie, I want you to do (this) today and I know you'll do a good job.'"

Nolan and others did do a good job, but the intermittent loss of manpower and equipment frustrated Fleming so much that he left the project before it was finished, allowing his son to button up the job.

Fleming, though, came back just before the course was officially opened and played a round with Nolan and others. Afterward, he gave it his approval.

While Fleming may have brought McLaren to life, Erik de Lambert, a quirky Swedish immigrant who ran Gleneagles for twenty-five years, resuscitated it.

De Lambert is an eccentric sort, with a love of Scotland so deep some say it borders on psychosis. Many around the bar swear that after his annual sojourn to Scotland, de Lambert returned to Gleneagles with such a thick Scottish accent he was nearly unintelligible.

It was de Lambert, a solid player in his own right, who changed the name of McLaren to Gleneagles International Golf Course, saying it reminded him of the Kings Course at Gleneagles Hotel Golf Club in Perthshire, Scotland. It was de Lambert who named the bar and pro shop "Old Peculiar"—the moniker Gleneagles regulars in turn bestowed on him. It was also de Lambert who made sure the bar was stocked with nearly twenty-five varieties of Scotch—mostly single malts—sold at the cheapest prices this side of Edinburgh. And most important of all, it was de Lambert who injected his attitude into Gleneagles.

When he ran the course from 1979 until 2004, anyone walking into the bar wearing sneakers with a demeanor that did not suit de Lambert would not be allowed to play for reasons of safety—sneakers didn't afford enough traction on the hilly course. But if a person with the indefinable right attitude walked through the door wearing sneakers and inquired about playing, de Lambert would retreat to a back room, reappearing with a pair of spikes in just the right size.

While some may view de Lambert as a curmudgeon, all will tell you he was the man who saved the course.

In 1979, City Hall decided it no longer wanted to be in the business of running golf courses, deciding to make McLaren the first course it leased out. The layout had nearly closed a few years earlier when a citywide strike by gardeners, including golf course maintenance workers, left the course unattended for weeks. It was only the efforts of the pro at the time—who took it upon himself to mow greens—that allowed the course to remain open.

De Lambert, a commercial photographer, was awarded the contract to run the course because he was the only one who applied.

Three years later, de Lambert, under the guidance of architect Robert Muir Graves, made changes to the course, adding more than forty bunkers and bringing the total to about fifty. Some pot bunkers—de Lambert's tribute to Scotland—were later removed.

Only one alteration was frowned upon by the regulars, and it continues to rankle them to this day. For reasons that are not clear—and apparently without Graves' input—de Lambert relocated the first green, creating one that is benched uncomfortably into a hill and does not fit the low-key style of the other eight. Even with that faux pas, though, players laud de Lambert.

Architect Damian Pascuzzo joined the Graves firm in 1982 and recalls how de Lambert visited the office to ask for advice on proposed changes to Gleneagles. Many Saturday mornings, Graves and Pascuzzo would make the hour's drive to Gleneagles to get in a round.

"De Lambert was an amazing guy," Pascuzzo said. "He was stout, barrel-chested with a big mustache. I remember him out there mowing greens in a corduroy coat."

The two would often be joined by de Lambert for a few holes, after which he would invariably pick their brains over a post-round cocktail.

His tenure came to an end with his retirement in 2004. Since then, partners Tom Hsieh (pronounced Shea) and Craig Lipton have leased the course. Hsieh has played Gleneagles for nearly twenty years. He instantly credits de Lambert for saving Gleneagles and creating the unique atmosphere where regulars feel as if they have ownership of the course. Hsieh and his partner are doing everything the can to preserve "the culture," as Hsieh calls it, that embraces some and shuns others.

"No other public course in San Francisco has members that police themselves," he said. "At any of the other municipal courses, if a member told you to fix your divot, there would be a fight. It's a self-selecting golf course."

He is comfortable with the fact not everyone would enjoy Gleneagles.

"My parents golf four times a week," he said, laughing. "But I haven't taken them here."

Northwood

MacKenzie in the Redwoods

The photo is of Dr. Alister MacKenzie striding down the first fairway of the Old Course, driver tucked under his arm, architect and friend Max Behr by his side, looking into the distance. Perhaps he is surveying the expanse in front of him—his favorite golf course in the world. Perhaps he is just searching for his ball. Maybe, though, he is looking into the future. If so, could he ever have imagined his travels would have taken him to the redwood forests of northern California?

For MacKenzie, the golf architecture world began and ended with the Old Course. His book *The Spirit of St. Andrews* is largely dedicated to the design genius of the Old, the greatest course in the world.

He took the tenets of design with him into a course architecture career that began in England with Alwoodley Golf Club and passed through the Suez Canal to Argentina, Australia, and New Zealand. He would return to the British Isles to remodel such courses as Lahinch Golf Club in Ireland, then journey to the United States, where he worked in partnership with such notables as Bobby Jones in creating Augusta National, and Perry Maxwell on Crystal Downs Country Club in Michigan and Oklahoma City Golf Course. When he set up shop on the West Coast, MacKenzie formed a partnership with Robert Hunter, and the two went on to produce such notable California courses as Cypress Point Club and San Francisco Golf Club.

MacKenzie then traveled north of San Francisco and into the Russian River Valley to design nine holes amidst the towering redwoods, the likes of which he had never seen. They were far removed in both distance and environment from his ideal for a golf course site, the links land of the British Isles. Despite all that, it is easy to experience Northwood Golf Course and realize that the design theories that MacKenzie had embraced half a world away are still in force there among the massive trees along the Russian River.

There are no vast expanses and long views of far-off Scottish hills as there are at St. Andrews. Instead, frozen emerald rivers of fairways rise and fall, gently maneuvering their way through redwood canyons that extend more than 150 feet into the air, their tops seemingly brushing the clouds. The putting surfaces, perhaps a tenth of the size of those at the Old, possess many of the same characteristics as their much bigger, much older brothers. They can rise sharply and then descend easily into plateaus, the contours serving the dual purposes of rejecting poor approaches and embracing well-struck ones.

In his book *The Spirit of St. Andrews*, MacKenzie takes a stance counter to those of most of his contemporaries: he sees the use of trees on a golf course as a legitimate hazard. He understands the criticism that trees are not found on links land, but he counters the point, writing that "on an inland course the only way, except at the enormous expense of providing hazards as high as sand dunes, is by the use of trees in groups."

It is unlikely that MacKenzie ever encountered a sand dune as high as the trees of Northwood, but his use of them is at times masterful.

Rarely does a player feel claustrophobic during the round, but the trees are a constant factor if shots are mishit.

For more than twenty years as superintendent, Ed Bale—who is also part of the ownership group of Northwood—has scaled the mighty timber to trim limbs and keep the recovery shot a vital part of the game at the course.

He is not the first man to put saw and axe to the redwoods of the Russian River Valley. In fact, the logging industry is precisely the reason that the town of Guerneville exists. Most astounding is that the behemoths that give the course its character are actually second-growth trees, the ancient ones having been logged in the nineteenth century.

Rail beds were laid before roadbeds, and as a result the first golfers—and MacKenzie—came to the area by train.

Across the Russian River from the course is the Bohemian Grove, the site of the annual two-week summer retreat of the Bohemian Club, located in San Francisco and founded by newspapermen—with editors banned—looking to create a friendly

Since it opened in 1929, Northwood Golf Course has drawn celebrities because of its location near the Bohemian Grove. Before roads were built, many of the famous and rich who made the trek to the Grove stayed in their own railcars. (Courtesy of Northwood Golf Course)

environment for artisans, writers, and painters. Ironically, the Bohemian Club has since become a haven for the rich and powerful of California. Up until the early 1990s, the membership of the male-only club was almost exclusively conservative, but that has changed—Jimmy Carter belongs. Every Republican president from Harry Truman forward has been a Bohemian. The majority of the members are from California; others come from across the United States and from nearly a dozen other countries.

Type "Bohemian Club" into any Internet search engine, and dozens of responses will pop up, many maintained by conspiracy theorists who expound on the club's rituals and symbols, all kept from the public eye. At least one doctoral thesis has been written on the group.

The organization was formed in 1872 in San Francisco for men who had a taste for art and literature. In the late 1870s, members began trekking to Sonoma County for a club get-together. Near the end of the century, the club began purchasing land in the area and today owns more than 2,700 acres, including hundreds of acres of redwoods.

Annually, most of the more than 2,000 members journey to the Bohemian Grove for two weeks of what amounts to a male-only frat party. The proceedings include the Cremation of Care ceremony, held on the banks of a manmade lake in front of a forty-foot concrete owl that serves as the club's symbol as well as a symbol of wisdom. While politics can be discussed during the sojourn, business cannot. In fact, the club's motto, "Weaving Spiders Come Not Here"—taken from William Shakespeare's *A Midsummer Night's Dream*—is even more strictly enforced at the Grove festivities.

Even into the 1960s, such entertainers as Bob Hope, Phil Harris, and Bing Crosby were a big part of the club. Harris even owned a home off the ninth green so he could partake in the Grove festivities but still have a quiet respite when needed. Now politicians and CEOs of major corporations and financial institutions dominate the membership.

One fact holds as true today as it did in the late 1920s—if Bohemian Club members wanted to golf, there was really only one choice: Northwood Golf Club.

It was the Bohemian connection that brought MacKenzie to Guerneville. John Neville, a talented amateur player in the Bay Area, was a Bohemian. He was a friend of MacKenzie, who by the late 1920s had come to California.

The influential members of the Bohemian Club most likely wanted the golf course, since there was little to do outside the Grove. The Russian River Valley at this point was still decades away from becoming a tourist area or a wine-producing region.

Opened in June of 1929, the course was called Rio Campo in a newspaper advertisement for the MacKenzie/Robert Hunter design firm. By the time *The Fairway* magazine wrote a piece on the opening in July of 1929, the name was already Northwood.

The Fairway had this to say: "The course is nine holes, all grass greens, tees, and fairways. The total distance of the nine holes is 3,181 yards. Fairways are bordered by redwoods, madrones, and pines, making the course very attractive for play and scenic beauty."

Interestingly, the original yardage was nearly 290 yards longer than that of the current layout.

Caddie Gaylord Schaap, eighteen when this photo was taken in 1940, with actor Aldophe Menjou to his left. Schaap is now one of a group of owners of the course, as is his son, Gaylord Schaap Jr., who is also the general manager. (Courtesy of Northwood Golf Course)

For nearly thirty years, the course fared well. Then, in 1958, a new road next to the fourth hole shortened it by about fifty yards; the dogleg right is now a touch over 290 yards. Five years later, in 1963, a massive flood that sent the Russian River over its banks wiped out the third green. A clubhouse expansion in 1975 shortened the first hole slightly, to just less than 300 yards.

The changes, though, could have been much worse. On two occasions, course owners nearly turned the layout into home lots.

The course's future was secured in 1970 when a group of nearly a dozen local businessmen purchased the layout. Included in that group was superintendent Ed Bale and his father, and general manager Gaylord Schaap and his father, Dr. Charles Schaap, who caddied at Northwood in the 1940s.

The series of previous owners had allowed the original layout to be softened; the worst transgression was the abandonment

of bunkers. Luckily, though, the intact footprints of the originals remain. They were not filled in, but turf grew over the sand.
Superintendent Bale has been carefully restoring some, reviv-
ing what surely is one the best unknown nine-hole golf courses
in the United States.

If the other bunkers are ever resurrected, Northwood will be
one of the half-dozen best nine-hole golf courses in the United
States; the first and sixth holes would easily stand as two of the
finest short par 4s in existence. And if Bale has his way, they
will be.

The first is a slight dogleg left with one of the few wide-open
tee shots of the round; the green and a bunker short right are
set in an amphitheater of big trees, visible from the tee.

In the center of the landing is a grassed-over fairway bunker
that, if returned, would make club members playing any of
MacKenzie's famous designs stand up and take notice. The bays
and fingers of the original are easily discerned. The floor is nearly
four feet below the top edge, meaning that a drive that found
the sand would all but eliminate any chance for an approach
able to reach the green.

Those looking to bomb a driver over the bunker must produce a nearly perfect effort. Redwoods on the left and forebod-
ing bunkers on the right, also in play on the sixth, sharply
penalize the shots that do not find fairway grass.

But even an approach shot from the middle of the fairway
calls for precision. The green is longer than it is wide, with the
front two-thirds a good two feet lower than the back plateau. A
wild hump on the right front can redirect a ball in myriad direc-
tions, landing it anywhere from the right rough to the back left
fringe. Two bunkers on the right side wait to penalize, as does
the drop-off that guards the left side of the green.

The first is paired perfectly with the sixth hole that borders
its right side. The first fairway, in fact, is a daring alternate way
to play the sixth, a 330-yard hard dogleg right that tempts players to carve a tee ball around the corner and directly at the
green. MacKenzie, however, threw up a gauntlet of hazards,
and only the most exact shots work.

The tee is set back into the redwoods, the row on the right
dissuading those thinking of playing a shot around the corner
into the first fairway. If that is not enough of a deterrent, an
artfully placed triad of bunkers along the right side also serves

The sixth at Northwood Golf Course looks the way it did on opening day in 1929. The fairway of the par-4 sixth is guarded on the left and right by bunkers. Playing in from the adjacent first fairway still means having to negotiate a greenside tree. (Courtesy of Northwood Golf Course)

the same purpose. A hefty bailout area is provided to the left, but a shot to the green from there forces an approach over a greenside bunker nestled into a narrow putting surface. Also in play is a left fairway bunker some forty yards short of the green.

The intrepid golfer may think of threading a tee ball through the trees and onto the first fairway—and Bale says there are some such golfers—but MacKenzie counters that strategy.

To defend his hole, MacKenzie placed a large bunker to the right of the green and then added a cherry tree on the outside of the bunker, so close that it overhangs the sand, creating a double hazard and forcing players to carry the tree to reach the green.

A black-and-white photo taken when the course was still young proves that it was MacKenzie's intent to guard the green complex with the bushy tree, which stands out from the surrounding behemoths.

The 382-yard second hole at Northwood, an Alister MacKenzie design, is cut out of a redwood forest and ends at a semi-punchbowl green not visible from the fairway. (Photograph by Sean Tully)

In *The Spirit of St. Andrews,* he articulated his thinking this way: "Groups of trees are the most effective way of preventing players reaching the green with their second shots after playing their drives in the wrong direction. No bunker guarding the green seem to be able to prevent them doing so."

Again, as on the first hole, MacKenzie requires thought and skill on the tee ball, coupled with a deadly accurate approach, as the only means of achieving par or better on a short par 4.

On the second hole he dips into a hole design commonly used in the British Isles—the punchbowl—but with a twist. Where usually the green is backstopped to create the bowl effect, at Northwood MacKenzie nestled the putting surface into a hollow that drops off at the back. A shoulder to the right and a down slope in front makes the bowl. The green sits well below fairway level so that only the top of the flag is visible on the approach shot.

The par-5 seventh, unofficially known as Charlie's Hole, adds more character to Northwood.

Just beyond the back of the green, longtime member Charlie Everett carved bears out of two large stumps. A golf hat usually winds up on one or both, and it is not uncommon for a group of newcomers to wait in the fairway for the rather large twosome on the green to putt out.

On the par-5 ninth, again using the contours provided, MacKenzie produced a daunting test to bring Northwood to its conclusion. The uphill tee shot is to a fairway that sits on the old railway track bed. At one time, fairway bunkers were artfully placed in the landing areas, making the finishing hole diabolical. Now only bunkers at the green remain.

Once you are at Northwood, it is easy to find plenty of reasons to stay and become immersed in the slower pace of the Russian River Valley. The small, cozy town of Guerneville is a short car ride away, but there is really no reason to leave the golf course. Off the same parking lot as the pro shop are a restaurant, a coffee shop, a post office, and the simple yet comfortable Northwood Lodge, where rooms have neither phones nor televisions. Since there is no cell phone service in the area, the laid-back atmosphere makes it that much easier to enjoy northern California's best nine-hole golf experience.

Acknowledgments

First of all, thanks to the good people at Ann Arbor Media Group.

Thanks to Larry Aylward and Tom Skernivitz at Golfdom, who covered for me and extended an incredible amount of patience when research for this book took over my life; Brad Klein, who brought me back to writing and into the world of golf course architecture; Bob Labbance; Geoff Shackelford; George Bahto for giving me so many headaches; Brett Zimmerman for the use of his camera and computer skills; Becca Adams and her fax machine; Patty Moran of the USGA library for her infinite patience with all my questions and requests; Tim Moraghan; and the members of the USGA Green Sections, especially Jim Skorulski; Turk Pipkin, Larry Lambrecht, Frank S. Rossi, and Ron Whitten.

Also thanks to Joe D'Ambrosio for introducing me to Fenwick Golf Course, Dave Cook for taking me to Fishers Island, the members of the St. Andrews Golf Club for allowing me the honor of membership, Doug Stein and King Oemig for allowing me to be part of the Seth Raynor Society, Kyle Zimmerman and Lauren Giordano for crashing through the brush in search of Ocean Links, Raymund Haddock, Sean Tully, Rick Lund, volunteer researcher Jim Arn and the staff of the Amateur Athletic Federation Library of Los Angeles, Tinted Blue, David Patrick Columbia, Harpoon Brewery, Tim Woodcock–security, and, of course, Terri Carta and Kris Overton.

Prairie Dunes: P. Stan George, Charles Craig, Randy Hunt, the owners and staff at Roy's BBQ.

Marion Golf Course: Paul Boutin (every course should be so lucky to have someone who cares so much about the history), Sue and Bruce Carlson for preserving that history, the helpful and patient staff of the Plymouth County, Massachusetts Registrar of Deeds.

Midway Golf Course: Kris Lindenberger and Jerry's Café in Inman.

Highland Links: Stewart Eyman, Susan Kurtzman and staff at the Truro Historical Society, the National Parks Service, especially Bill Burke, Melissa Lewandowski and Larry Lowenthal (ret.).

Ocean Links: Jean Tailer, Toni Tailer Smith, Fern Tailer DeNavares, Patrick Hayes Jr., Barclay Douglas, Dick Masse and the Rhode Island Park Service, Bert Lippincott and the staff of the Newport Historical Society, Dave Donatelli for rediscovering and preserving a bit of history.

Fenwick Golf Course: Ellsworth Grant, The Old Saybrook Historical Society, especially Martha Soper.

Gleneagles: Tom Hsieh, William Smith, Ignacio Aramburo, San Francisco Convention and Visitors Bureau, Steve Proctor, the staff of the Phoenix Hotel, Will McCulloch.

Wawona Hotel Golf Course: Monica Miller, Kim Porter, Linda Eade and Barbara Beroza at the Yosemite National Park Service Research Library, Tom Bopp.

Sewanee Golf Course: Mark Webb, Dan Hatfield, Dale Mooney.

Whitinsville Golf Club: Chris Hulme, David Johnson.

Northwood Golf Club: Ed Bale, Gaylord Schaap, Northwood Lodge.

Rolling Rock Club: John Yakubisin, Stephen J. Klee, and the Pie Shoppe of Ligonier

I want to especially thank the superintendents and architects who have taken the time to answer my questions and enlighten me on the art of their crafts, especially Herb Watson and the entire greenkeeping staff of the Hartford Golf Club, Euan Grant and the staffs of the St. Andrews, Scotland golf courses; Keith Angilly, Donnie Beck and his staff, Paul Sabino, Mike Echols, Karl Olsen, Tim Davis, Roby Robertson IV, Brian Peterson, Scott Wicker, Mark Stovall, Scott Ramsay, Michael Stackowicz, Charles Martineau, Craig Currier, Mark Michaud, Chuck and Jackie Welch, Brian Barrington, Jon Jennings for getting me that book I really needed, Paul Miller, Phil Neaton, David Heroian, Kip Tyler, Pat Sisk, Dan Dinelli, Pat Kriksceonaitis, and architects Brian Silva, Mark Mungeam, Tim Gerrish for the drawing, Brian Johnson, Steve Smyers, Gil Hanse, Ron

Forse, Tom Doak, Jack Nicklaus, Brad Booth, Brad Faxon, Steven Kay, and Robert Trent Jones II.

There are friends for whom a simple thank-you in a book will never convey my deep appreciation for the help and support they have given me: Scott Vangel, Bonnie Phillips, Eddie Adams, Jeff Burt and Donna Scaglione, Maryann Beckett, Bill Giering, Geoff Childs, Joe and Wilma MacMillan, Stacy and Nick Chiocchio, Rich White, George Ruhe, and Michael Haymes.